Faith
that
Works

STUDIES IN THE
EPISTLE OF JAMES

New Testament Studies

Faith
that
Works

STUDIES IN THE
EPISTLE OF JAMES

HOMER ◆ A ◆ KENT, JR.

BAKER BOOK HOUSE
Grand Rapids, Michigan 49506

To **Brian Kent Woolman**
with the love of your proud grandfather,
and the prayer
that you will always be quick to hear
the Word of God

James 1:19

Contents

Illustrations

Abbreviations

Arndt	*A Greek-English Lexicon of the New Testament,* by William F. Arndt and F. Wilbur Gingrich.
ASV	American Standard Version, 1901
EBC	*The Expositor's Bible Commentary*
EGT	*The Expositor's Greek Testament*
ICC	International Critical Commentary series
KJV	King James Version, 1611
LXX	Septuagint (Greek translation of the Old Testament)
NASB	New American Standard Bible, 1971
Nestle-Aland	*Novum Testamentum Graece*
NICNT	New International Commentary of the New Testament series
NIGTC	New International Greek Testament Commentary series
NIV	New International Version, 1973
NT	New Testament
OT	Old Testament
TDNT	*Theological Dictionary of the New Testament*
TNTC	Tyndale New Testament Commentaries series
UBS	United Bible Societies Greek New Testament

Foreword

To have been the oldest half-brother of God's incarnate Son; to have lived with Him for thirty years in Nazareth as an unbeliever; to have been the recipient of a special post-resurrection appearance of his Savior; to have served for thirty years as the pastor-teacher of the mother church of Jerusalem; and to have suffered a martyr's death—all of these astounding descriptions apply to the author of this inspired New Testament document.

Should we not listen carefully to the Holy Spirit's message to us through this "general" Epistle to *all* Christians of the church age?

Close and prolonged study of the Book of James has led one recent commentator, James B. Adamson, to conclude that "James was a master writer whose knowledge and choice of Greek bestow on his epistle a sustained unity of style and content which bears a close affinity with the Synoptic Gospels and the sayings of Jesus. The substance and authoritative tone of the Epistle follow in the tradition of Elijah and Moses, and the style and diction resemble some of the outstanding qualities of the Psalms and Prophets."

Dr. Homer A. Kent, Jr., a devoted and skillful student of God's Word, and a colleague for thirty-five years at Grace Theological Seminary, has served the church of his generation well in his various New Testament commentaries. They have been widely received because they are based on a reverent, meticulous, and balanced interpretation of the original text of the New Testament.

This commentary is no exception. For a sample of the freshness and relevance of his analysis, see chapter 13 on James 5:13–20 ("Sickness and Sinning") concerning the anointing of the sick with oil. Roman Catholic "extreme unction" and modern "faith healing" interpretations are carefully refuted, and a consistent biblical view is presented, much to the potential encouragement of God's suffering people.

I heartily recommend this study of a relatively neglected but exceedingly precious portion of the inspired Word of God. May the Book of James thereby become even more appreciated as a "perfect gift from above, coming down from the Father of lights" to illumine and bless many hearts in these days of testing and trouble.

John C. Whitcomb

Preface

The Epistle of James may be the oldest book in the New Testament, but its message is as fresh as tomorrow morning. Careful reading of its content in a clear translation communicates a challenge to an active faith that every Christian should find relevant. The themes discussed are intensely human, and James was a graphic and compelling writer who gives evidence of experience as a dramatic preacher.

Martin Luther's oft-quoted comment that James is a "right strawy epistle" should not be isolated from its context. Luther was comparing James with the foundational works of doctrine, such as John's Gospel, Romans, Galatians, and 1 Peter. He noted that James does not deal with such matters and thus does not have that particular "evangelical nature" in it. However, Christians through the centuries have found that James describes life on the plane where most believers live it—on the routine and mundane level where faith and living join in daily experience.

The studies in this volume have grown out of the writer's experience in teaching James for many years at Grace Theological Seminary, and in preaching its themes in Bible conferences and churches. It is his understanding that James the author was the half-brother of Jesus, that his Epistle is a Christian document, and that it properly belongs in the canon of Scripture.

Hearty thanks go to three faculty colleagues: to John Whitcomb, who wrote the foreword; and to John Sproule and George Zemek, who read the manuscript and assisted with helpful suggestions. A special word of appreciation belongs to Nancy Weimer, the author's faithful secretary for more than eight years, who typed the manuscript.

Homer A. Kent, Jr.
Winona Lake, Indiana

1

Introduction to the Epistle

The Epistle of James may be the first New Testament document to have been written. It is surely the oldest surviving epistolary glimpse into Jewish Christianity. Written to Jewish churches outside of Palestine from a Jewish-Christian perspective within Palestine, it shows us what the earliest Christian churches were like, what problems they grappled with, and what solutions were appropriate. The letter belongs with those other Jewish-Christian documents, Hebrews and the Petrine Epistles, as a reflection of early Christian life among those whose ancestral traditions had been rooted in Mosaic law and Jewish culture. Even though the Christian faith knows no racial or cultural barriers, every man is influenced by his culture and his upbringing. A recognition of the background of the Epistle of James helps the reader to understand more fully the overtones of the problems being discussed and the nuances conveyed in the argumentation.

The author of this Epistle was a forceful and dramatic communicator, not unlike his half-brother Jesus. His imagery is colorful and frequent. His illustrations are drawn from nature and commonplace experiences. His themes are practical, not theoretical. He dealt with people and their immediate needs, and he was clearly in touch with human problems.

The Epistle of James is a clear example of what was involved as early Christians "were continually devoting themselves to the apostles' teaching" (Acts 2:42). What began as oral instruction to the early church in Jerusalem soon came to be written and circulated among Christian assemblies throughout the world. The basic challenges that confronted Christian living in the first century were little different from those of today. Whether the audience is Jewish or Gentile, if it is Christian the Epistle of James speaks with equal force and clarity as it directs men's lives along scriptural patterns.

Authorship

The Traditional View: James, the Lord's Brother

Although the Epistle itself states James to be its author (1:1), it does not distinguish him from several who bore this common name. Consequently, numerous suggestions have been offered as candidates for authorship. The most widely held view, however, ascribes the writing to James, the Lord's brother (i.e., James the Just).

Evidence that this identification is correct, while not conclusive, is nevertheless strong. This James is consistently referred to by his personal name alone, as in 1:1 (see Matt. 13:55; Acts 12:17; 15:13, 21:18; Gal. 2:9, 12; Jude 1). The other Jameses in the New Testament have some additional designation to identify them (see Matt. 4:21; 10:3; Acts 12:2). Only a very prominent person could use such a common name without further identification. To suggest some obscure "James" would not be convincing.

Furthermore, the headship of the Jerusalem church—a position that James, the Lord's brother, seems to have held following the departure of the Twelve for their various ministries—gave him contact with Jewish Christians from many places.[1] Visitors to the

1. Indication of James's leadership at Jerusalem is found in Acts 12:17; 15:13–21; 21:18; Gal. 2:9, 12.

Christian community in Jerusalem may well have kept in touch with James after they returned to their homes in the Diaspora, and this letter would be an instance of that continuing contact (1:1). This position would also have given him the prominence that this James obviously had.

The beginning of the Epistle also agrees with the letter prepared at the Jerusalem Conference (Acts 15), where James seems to have presided. The common contemporary greeting[2] employed in 1:1 is used by no other New Testament Epistle, but it is found in the letter that James undoubtedly had a large part in composing to the Gentile readers who lived among the Diaspora (Acts 15:23).

Certain problems, however, have been raised with this traditional view. If the Epistle was written by this well-known James, why was there such a delay in recognizing its canonical status? It is true that James was not included among the "acknowledged books" of Eusebius,[3] and it seems not to have been as well known in the West as in the East. The answer may be that it was written in Jerusalem for Jewish churches in the Eastern Diaspora and thus did not circulate as early and as widely in the West. Furthermore, it is possible that a neglect of James in favor of the more doctrine-centered Epistles, such as characterized the Reformation and much of present-day Christianity, may have also been true in the early centuries.

Another problem concerns the high quality of the Greek found in this Epistle. Moulton and Howard called it "perhaps the best Greek in the New Testament,"[4] although such judgments are admittedly subjective. The intimation is that a Galilean James would hardly have been capable of such literary skill. Yet it is clear that Galilee was bilingual, so there is no reason to suppose that

2. Greek: *chairein*.

3. Eusebius, *Ecclesiastical History* (London: Society for Promoting Christian Knowledge, 1927), III, 25, 3.

4. J. H. Moulton and W. F. Howard, *A Grammar of New Testament Greek* (Edinburgh: T. & T. Clark, 1929), II, 27.

James could not have been proficient in Greek. Perhaps he took over the family carpentry business after Jesus left for public ministry, and this could have propelled him to become proficient in Greek. The use of an amanuensis could have supplied some stylistic polish. However, a flair for dramatic and forceful communication has no geographical or academic limitations. A peasant from Galilee could be just as effective a communicator as one more highly educated. Any deficiencies in literary style could be rectified by the amanuensis. This, of course, does not dilute the Epistle's inspiration, for the author maintained full authority over the document. Both Paul (Rom. 16:22) and Peter (1 Peter 5:12) used amanuenses.

Although it is true that the author gave no hint that he was a half-brother of Jesus, such an objection may reflect more on our modern tendency to exploit "inside information" or special relationships. For one who eventually accepted Jesus' teaching (Matt. 12:46–50), even though at first he did not (John 7:5), a reticence to trade on family connections would be readily understandable.

Alternative Views

No attempt will be made here to delineate in detail the various alternative views of authorship that have been offered. Thorough discussions are readily available in the standard works on New Testament introduction.[5] A brief mention and evaluation of the more common ones will suffice.

To suggest a pseudonymous writer who employed the name of James raises more problems than it solves. It is not likely that a forger (regardless of his motives) would have identified himself as "James" without being more explicit as to which James. A forger

5. For instance, see Donald Guthrie, *New Testament Introduction,* or Everett F. Harrison, *Introduction to the New Testament* (1971).

Jerusalem, where James was the leader of the church and from which he presumably wrote his Epistle.

would not want to leave any loose ends that would prompt further inquiry. Furthermore, why would a writer need to cloak himself falsely with James's authority for a letter that contained no particular innovations?

To attribute authorship to either of the two Jameses among the Twelve (James of Alphaeus, James of Zebedee) encounters the objection that no positive evidence exists for either of these men as the writer. The author does not claim apostleship, and it is not likely that the simple "James" without further identification would have been immediately understood of either man. No early traditions support either identification.

A more bizarre explanation sees the Epistle in a somewhat allegorical fashion as built upon the "Jacob motif."[6] Inasmuch as "James" and "Jacob" are simply two renderings of the same name,

6. This theory was first proposed by Arnold Meyer, *Das Ratsel des Jakobusbriefes* (Giessen: A Jopelmann, 1930).

21

this explanation views the Epistle as patterned after Jacob's farewell to his twelve sons (Gen. 49). The name *James* is the equivalent of *Jacob* (1:1); the discussion of "joy" is related to the name *Isaac* (1:2); "patience" is related to *Rebecca* (1:3–4); "hearing" is somehow construed with *Simeon* (1:19–24). The theory is more clever than convincing and has enlisted very few supporters.

More recently, the methodology of redaction criticism that has been applied to the Gospels has been suggested as helpful in determining the authorship of the Epistle of James. This procedure entails considering the various units of the composition as being assembled in a certain way by a redactor or editor in order to accomplish his purpose. Peter H. Davids gives an extensive analysis of the various phenomena in this Epistle.[7] He argues that all the material in the letter came from James, but that it was edited at a somewhat later time (still in the first century) either by James or some member of the church.[8] He draws this conclusion from the many self-contained units of thought found in the letter without clear connection, the use of proverbial sayings to join differing sense units, and several other factors.[9] Davids summarizes his understanding in these words:

> This commentary assumes, then, that the original traditions appeared during the early part of this period, i.e. late 40s and early 50s. They were gathered together during the latter part to solidify the church's position. Thus the work is perhaps the last picture one has of the Palestinian church before the storms of war closed over it.[10]

Nevertheless, while providing explanation for many of the phenomena encountered in the letter, this theory is by no means

7. Peter Davids, *The Epistle of James*, NIGTC (Grand Rapids: Eerdmans, 1982), pp. 1–61.
8. Ibid., p. 22.
9. Ibid., pp. 22–23.
10. Ibid., p. 34.

convincing to all. Why should the presence of separate sense units, which are joined together only with difficulty, be a better argument for a redactor than for the original author? If this circumstance is viewed as a weakness, it would appear that the editor did a very poor job of providing transitions, inasmuch as the separate topics are clearly seen. For instance, Davids comments on 5:7–20: "Thus there is a merging of themes in this summary section and some disjointedness as the redactor pulls materials together, yet there is a real sense of unity with the rest of the book as themes are resumed and brought into dynamic relationship with one another."[11] He states regarding the presence of the wisdom passage (3:13–18) after the discussion on the tongue: "The redactor has not erred by including the paragraph in this place."[12] One wonders why it is necessary to assume a redactor at all. If James is predicated as the source of all the material, there is little to be gained by bringing an additional editor into the picture. Furthermore, serious questions can be raised regarding inspiration if editorial work is allowed apart from the author's personal inspection. Who was the human agent through whom the Holy Spirit inspired the Scripture? James or the redactor? The theory is interesting but hardly necessary to explain the data in James.

Theodore A. Hildebrandt demonstrated in a recent study that continuity patterns do exist in proverbial literature, even though a casual reading of the proverbs might suggest them to be haphazard collections.[13] It should occasion no surprise, therefore, if James's various topics were also found to have an inner connection, without resorting to a redactor.

---

11. Ibid., p. 181.
12. Ibid., p. 149.
13. Theodore A. Hildebrandt, *Proverbial Poetry: Its Settings and Syntax* (Grace Theological Seminary: unpublished dissertation, 1985).

The Life of James

Accepting the traditional view of authorship, one may discover from Scripture a modest amount of background information about James. He was the half-brother of Jesus, the child of Joseph and Mary (Gal. 1:19).[14] Because he is mentioned first in the list of the Lord's brothers, it may be concluded that he was next in age after Jesus (Matt. 13:55; Mark 6:3). James was presumably still a member of the family circle when Jesus and the family moved from Nazareth to Capernaum shortly after the start of the Lord's public ministry (Matt. 4:13; John 2:12).

During Christ's ministry, James, along with his brothers and mother, tried to visit Jesus (Matt. 12:46–50; Mark 3:31–35; Luke 8:19–21). Perhaps they were concerned about His health because of His strenuous activity and the reports that were circulating (Mark 3:21–31). Until at least seven months before the crucifixion, however, James remained an unbeliever in Jesus' mission (John 7:3–5).

When Jesus rose from the dead, James was the recipient of a special post-resurrection appearance (1 Cor. 15:7). Was this the occasion of his conversion? Later we find him in the upper room at Jerusalem, along with Mary, His brothers, and the disciples who were waiting for the Holy Spirit as Jesus had promised (Acts 1:14).

As the Jerusalem church became established, James is found in an increasingly prominent role. Paul visited him on his first post-conversion trip to Jerusalem, and this may imply that James

14. Efforts to make James a foster brother of Jesus (older son of the widower Joseph who later married the Virgin Mary) are rooted in the ancient attempts to protect the perpetual virginity of Mary. Such an explanation is without any reliable historical foundation. The view that Jesus and James were cousins is based upon a most uncertain identification of this James with James the son of Alphaeus. A variation of this theory identifies Alphaeus with Clopas and calls him a brother of Joseph.

himself was an apostle, at least in the wider sense (Gal. 1:18–19). He calls him one of the "pillars," along with Peter and John (Gal. 2:9). Peter, upon his miraculous release from prison, asked that the news be conveyed specifically to James, as well as to others (Acts 12:17). James emerges as the leader of the Jerusalem Conference (Acts 15:13–21). When certain tradition-minded Jewish Christians came to Antioch, apparently from the church at Jerusalem, Paul said they were "from James," presumably because they had come from the church where he was the leader (Gal. 2:12). Later, when Paul visited Jerusalem at the end of his third missionary journey, he made his report to James and the elders (Acts 21:18). This manner of referring to James strongly implies that he was the leader of the Jerusalem congregation.

Several references outside the New Testament testify to James's piety and devotion to the Jewish law. In the writings of Hegesippus (ca. A.D. 180), James is depicted as a Nazarite whose times of prayer for his nation were so frequent and prolonged that his knees became calloused like the knees of a camel.[15]

Other traditions identify him as the first "bishop" of Jerusalem.[16] The death of James is recorded by the first-century historian Josephus, who said he was stoned to death on orders of the Sadducean high priest Ananus.[17] Another account of his death is given by Hegesippus, who said James was asked to give his understanding of Jesus. When he said that Jesus was the Son of man, seated at the right hand of God, he was thrown down from the temple, stoned, and then killed with a club.[18]

---

15. Quoted by Eusebius, *Ecclesiastical History,* 2.23. *The Ante-Nicene Fathers,* edited by Alexander Roberts and James Donaldson (repr. 1978), VIII, 762.

16. Clement of Alexandria, quoted by Eusebius, *Ecclesiastical History,* 2.1.3. Eusebius, *The Ecclesiastical History and The Martyrs of Palestine,* trans. Hugh Jackson Lawlor and John E. L. Oulton (London, 1928), II, 59.

17. Josephus, *Antiquities of the Jews,* 20.9 (197–203), trans. Louis H. Feldman, The Loeb Classical Library (Cambridge: Harvard Univ. Press, 1965), pp. 495–96.

18. Hegesippus, quoted by Eusebius. *The Ante-Nicene Fathers,* VIII, 763.

Original Readers

Although some have attempted to make a case for Christians generally as the original readers,[19] information from the letter itself, coupled with the lack of any clear contradictory evidence, argues strongly that Jewish Christians are in view. The letter is addressed to "the twelve tribes who are dispersed abroad" (i.e., the Diaspora, 1:1). Only by spiritualizing this very common technical expression for Jews living outside of Palestine can this be interpreted of "spiritual Israel" or Christendom. However, it must also be noted that the readers in view are not Jews in general but Christian Jews. They are ones who hold "faith in our glorious Lord Jesus Christ." (2:1), while at the same time perhaps being a nucleus within a larger synagogue setting.

Furthermore, their regular meeting place is called a "synagogue"[20] (2:2), the regular term for the Jewish religious assembly. It is also called a "church" in 5:14, but that designation was also a common usage among Jewish Christians (Acts 5:11; 8:1, 3:11–22).

It is true, however, that this is a Christian document. Inasmuch as there is no difference in Christ between Jew and Gentile, one may expect to find no instruction in this Epistle that does not pertain equally well to every Christian regardless of his background. The only real significance of identifying the original readers as Jewish is the help it provides in understanding the background out of which those readers were confronting and responding to this Christian instruction.

19. A. E. Barnett, "James, Letter of," *The Interpreter's Dictionary of the Bible,* (New York: Abingdon, 1962), E–J, 795.

20. Greek: *synagōgē*

Date of the Epistle

The Epistle of James has no explicit indicators of the date of its composition. Nevertheless, there are some features about the letter that make an early date probable.

1. Many references to Christ's teachings are found, but there is little exact verbal agreement with the Gospels. An extensive list is given by Guthrie.[21] Some clear examples are the mentions of oathtaking (5:12, cf. Matt. 5:34–37), peacemakers (3:18, cf. Matt. 5:9), and judging (4:11–12, cf. Matt. 7:1–5). Apparently the author did not quote from our written Gospels, even though this was common practice after they were written. This factor suggests the Epistle James to have been written prior to the Gospels.

2. Considerable attention is given in the letter to the economic inequity between the poor and the rich among the readers. This condition largely ceased after the Roman-Jewish War (A.D. 66–70), a fact suggesting that the Epistle appeared before the war.

3. A very simple ecclesiastical organization is reflected in the letter. Only elders are mentioned when the sick are instructed as to procedures to be followed (5:14). None of the second-century tendency toward more elaborate administration is evident.

4. An eager expectancy of Christ's return appears in the letter (5:3, 7–9). Such expectation was prevalent in the early church and thus is a mark of an early date. Unfortunately this eagerness became weaker in later centuries.

5. No hint is given of the Jewish-Gentile controversy that occupied so large a place among the churches from the time of the Jerusalem Conference (A.D. 49–50) through the next several decades. Paul's Epistles have much to say about the matter. It is

21. Donald Guthrie, *New Testament Introduction, Hebrews to Revelation* (Chicago: Inter-Varsity, 1962), pp. 67–68.

27

difficult to imagine that James would not have felt impelled to mention it among the issues affecting Jewish-Christian conduct if it had already surfaced. Consequently a date in the 40s is reasonable, making it perhaps the earliest New Testament document.

6. On the assumption that James, the Lord's brother, was the author, the latest possible date of writing would have been in the 60s. Josephus places the death of James at about A.D. 62, and Hegesippus assigns a time at approximately A.D. 66.[22]

Place of Writing

Nothing in the letter itself is decisive regarding the author's location when he wrote. James, however, exercised his entire ministry in Jerusalem, and thus he presumably wrote his Epistle either in that city or somewhere else in Palestine. The illustrations he uses, especially those drawn from nature, fit that geographical location very well (for instance, 1:10–11; 3:11–12; 5:7).

Characteristics

Certain features about the letter make it distinctive in the New Testament. The student would do well to note these and other characteristics so that James will be recognized for its unique contribution to the New Testament collection.

1. It is the most Jewish book of the New Testament. Except for a very few references (primarily 1:1, 2:1), the Epistle would fit

---

22. See notes 16 and 17.

easily into the Old Testament literature. This is not to suggest that it is not thoroughly Christian but rather that it meshes easily with the concepts and activity with which godly Jews lived.

2. This letter contains no teaching on redemption through the death of Christ. It does not deny it; it simply does not discuss it.

3. Although it is a letter, it is quite impersonal. No greetings are sent to individuals, no personal references are made regarding either the author or any readers, and only the most general descriptions of situations are given. Although this can be largely accounted for by the circumstance that it was a "general" or perhaps circular letter going to many churches (1:1), the fact remains that there are no personal references.

4. Many references to nature characterize the author's literary style. James speaks about the billowing of the sea (1:6), wind (1:6, 11; 3:4), the sun (1:11, 17), grass and flowers (1:11), horses (3:3) and other animals, birds, and sea creatures (3:7), springs (3:11), figs, olives, and grapevines (3:12), agriculture (5:7), and rain (5:17–18).

5. A number of teachings in James are similar to Christ's, especially to the Sermon on the Mount, even though James does not state them exactly like Matthew's record in chapters 5 to 7.

6. The Greek is of high quality.

7. The approach in the letter emphasizes the practical aspects of Christian commitment. James's purpose was clearly to show that Christian faith was to demonstrate itself through godly living.

Outline of James

I. Greeting (1:1)
II. Trials and Temptations (1:2–27)
   A. The Christian's Attitude Toward Trials from Without (1:2–12)

1. He should count the experience of trials to be joy (1:2)
2. He should recognize the good results of trials (1:3–4)
3. He should ask God for wisdom to deal with trials (1:5–8)
4. Both poor and rich Christians should glory in their spiritual position (1:9–11)
5. He should look forward to the reward of successful testing (1:12)

B. The Christian's Attitude Toward Temptation from Within (1:13–27)
1. The source of sinful temptation (1:13–16)
2. The remedy for sinful temptation (1:17–18)
3. The Christian's responsibility (1:19–27)

III. Favoritism (2:1–13)
A. The Exhortation to Avoid Favoritism (2:1)
B. The Illustration from the Christian Assembly (2:2–4)
C. The Argument Against Favoritism (2:5–11)
1. It is inconsistent with God's action (2:5)
2. It is inappropriate in view of man's actions (2:6–7)
3. It is a transgression of the royal law (2:8–11)
D. Conclusion (2:12–13)

IV. Faith and Works (2:14–26)
A. Faith Without Works Is Dead (2:14–19)
1. It brings no salvation to its possessor (2:14)
2. It gives no help to others (2:15–16)
3. It offers no evidence that it lives (2:17–19)
B. Faith That Works Is True Faith (2:20–26)
1. The probing question (2:20)
2. Two biblical illustrations (2:21–25)
3. The sober conclusion (2:26)

V. Teachers and the Tongue (3:1–18)
A. The Importance of the Tongue (3:1–5a)
1. The exhortation (3:1–2)
2. The illustrations (3:3–5a)
B. The Dangers of the Tongue (3:5b–12)

C. Converting a Sinner (5:19–20)
  1. The sinner restored (5:19)
  2. The benefits achieved (5:20)

Questions for Discussion

1. What are the factors that help us decide which James is the author of this Epistle?
2. What are the reasons for understanding that James was written very early in the Christian era?
3. Why was James an appropriate person to write to Jewish Christians in the Diaspora?
4. What conclusions can you draw about first-century Jewish churches from the Epistle of James?
5. What special features come to your mind when you think of the Epistle of James?

2
Trials—The Testing from Without

James 1:1–12

In this perhaps earliest of New Testament books to be written, it is not too surprising that it tells us how to live. Because the Christian faith is not just an organization to join or a few abstract doctrines to hold, a letter like James's is immediately relevant to every Christian. Becoming a Christian introduces one into a new life that must then be lived. The Christian faith requires each believer to bring every thought and action into conformity to the Word of God. It proclaims a Christian philosophy of life in stark contrast to the self-seeking, unfocused, and often tumultuous existence that frequently characterizes those outside the faith.

This totally practical letter was written to meet the needs of ordinary people. The readers were not aristocrats but common folks. They were not Jewish Christians of Palestine but were dispersed in other places. Furthermore, it is obvious from the topics discussed that they were not always victorious in their Christian lives, and some may not have been genuine Christians at all.

A matter worth pondering is the fact that the very first topic James discussed involved the difficulties encountered in the Christian life. Totally foreign to him was the curious modern notion that becoming a Christian will make life easier, that all problems will disappear, and that the prospect in this life for each believer is that he will live "happily ever after." It is quite true that the Christian life should be satisfying. However, it is not satisfying because of the absence of difficulties but rather because the believer who knows the Scripture can face difficulties from a new perspective. It is this perspective that James conveys to his readers in his remarkable letter.

I. Greetings (1:1)

In the usual pattern of first-century letters, the author identifies himself and then designates his readers. Here the author is James, the brother of Jesus and also of Jude (see further discussion in chapter 1, "Introduction to the Epistle"). Only in this letter and the Epistle of Jude are the writers identified simply as "bond-servant" (Greek: *doulos*). These men were sufficiently well known in the Christian community that they did not need to claim any official position. Nor did they wish to trade on their blood relation to Jesus. At the same time, they were not part of the Twelve, so they did not call themselves "apostles of Jesus Christ."

By designating himself as a bondservant of "God and the Lord Jesus Christ," James has put Jesus and God the Father on the same plane,[1] surely a remarkable statement for a half-brother to

---

1. A similar coupling of God and the Lord Jesus Christ occurs in 2 Peter 1:2, where it is evident that *theou* refers to the Father, not to *Iēsou tou Kuriou*. Hence the reference is most probably to two persons in James 1:1. It is not an instance of Granville Sharp's first rule (which would require an article), but of Sharp's fifth rule which states: "And also when there is no article before the first noun, the insertion of the copulative *kai* before the next noun, or name, of the same case, denotes a different person or thing from the first...." Although Sharp later changed his mind about James 1:1 and was willing to call it an exception rather

make. Only if James had been convinced of the deity of Jesus Christ could such a statement have been made.

The letter was addressed to "the twelve tribes which are in the Diaspora" (cf. 1 Peter 1:1, author's trans.). The designation "twelve tribes" was a common designation of the Israelite nation (Acts 26:7). Apparently there were no "lost tribes" in James's estimation. More specifically, these were Jewish people who lived outside of Palestine. The term *Diaspora* (NASB, "dispersed") was a technical designation of Jews who lived among the Gentiles (John 7:35). It was used frequently in that sense in the Greek version of the Old Testament.[2] Inasmuch as this was such a well-known designation, and there is no problem with understanding it in that sense here, it is best to interpret it in this way. James, as leader of the Jerusalem church, could easily write to Jewish Christians who would quite naturally look to Jerusalem for their spiritual guidance. Perhaps many of them had visited with him in Jerusalem. If the early date of this Epistle is accepted (see chapter 1), it was written even before Paul's first missionary journey. At that time the vast majority of Christians were Jews, including those in the Gentile world. Thus the address to Christian Jews is not surprising. To explain the greeting as a metaphorical reference to all Christians who are scattered and away from their heavenly home is not warranted by the data.

"Greetings" was a common expression in first-century letters, although it appears in no other New Testament canonical Epistle.[3] It does occur in two letters recorded in Acts (15:23; 23:26).

---

than an example of rule five, there appears no strong reason not to treat it as a clear example of the rule. Granville Sharp, *Remarks on the Uses of the Definitive Article in the Greek Test of the New Testament* (Philadelphia: B. B. Hopkins, 1807), pp. 11–13.

2. See LXX, Deut. 28:25; 30:4, Jer. 41:17.

3. Greek: *chairein*. Grammatically it is an imperatival infinitive.

II. Trials and Temptations (1:2–27)

A. The Christian's Attitude Toward Trials from Without (1:2–12)

1. He should count the experience of trials to be joy (1:2)

James wasted no time in coming to an unpleasant subject and ordering a most difficult response. They were to "consider it all joy" whenever they encountered various trials. The trials (*peirasmois*) in view here are outward circumstances that one "encounters." This latter term (*peripesēte*) is the one used of the man who fell among thieves (Luke 10:30). The trials envisioned are therefore not sinful experiences but are tests to strengthen the believer. Neither are they seen here as inward spiritual conflicts. They are rather the situations that James assumed would occur to every Christian at some time or other and that could take a variety of forms (*poikilois*). They need not always be in the form of persecution, although that was frequently the case in the early church.

To "consider it all joy" means to respond with a deliberate intelligent appraisal, not an emotional reaction. A Christian is to look at the experience from God's perspective and recognize the trial not as a happy experience in itself but as the means of producing something most valuable. To consider it "all joy" is to see nothing bad in it at all. The trial itself is not called a joy, but the encounter is.

2. He should recognize the good results of trials (1:3–4)

VERSE 3. The believer must raise his eyes above the immediate unpleasantness of the trial and find joy in what God will accomplish by it. The same thought is expressed by Paul (Rom. 5:3–5).

This expression, "the testing of your faith," can be understood in two ways. If "testing" (*dokimion*) is treated as a noun, the rendering in most English versions is appropriate. The thought would be that the experience of having one's faith tested will produce a greater patience or endurance. However, the term can be understood as a neuter adjective (meaning "proven, tested, genuine") used substantively. Hence the translation would be "that which is genuine in your faith" or "the genuineness of your faith."[4] In the only other New Testament occurrence of this word (1 Peter 1:7), this translation yields far better sense. In either instance James was making the point that the presence of trials in the lives of believers refines their faith so that what is false can be stripped away and the genuine part that continues to trust God will develop victorious positive endurance.

The virtue that trials can help Christians develop is endurance (*hupomonēn*). When this term is translated "patience" (e.g., KJV), it sometimes suggests a passive resignation to unpleasant situations. However, the term is not a negative but a positive one. It describes the person who bravely remains upright and firm under adverse circumstances, without collapse or cowardice. Such translations as "steadfastness," "perseverance," or "brave endurance" are therefore preferable. The word was used by Paul to describe his own performance of apostolic signs in the midst of opposition (2 Cor. 12:12). It described the endurance with which Christ faced His enemies (2 Thess. 3:5). James used the word later in this letter to describe Job's continuing faith in God in spite of the most crushing troubles (5:11).

VERSE 4. Without this quality, believers are not "perfect and complete." The first term denotes something fully grown or mature (*teleioi*). Absence of this spiritual characteristic of steadfastness in trials is an indication that the believer is still a

4. Adolf Deissmann, *Bible Studies,* trans. Alexander Grieve (Edinburgh: T. & T. Clark, 1901), pp. 259–262.

spiritual infant, not as fully developed as he ought to be. The second term describes something that is whole, having all its parts, undamaged (*holokleroi*). It adds to the thought that just as a person may be full grown but minus a leg or lame in some way,[5] so a believer may be spiritually mature in other respects but not really complete if he has no steadfastness in adversity. Trials in the Christian life should cause us to trust God more and thus bring about the bracing and discipline that is necessary for vigorous growth. Christ Himself was made "perfect" through suffering (Heb. 2:10). He learned patient obedience by the things that He suffered (Heb. 5:8).

3. He should ask God for wisdom to deal with trials (1:5–8)

VERSE 5. By picking up the word "lacking" from verse 4, James indicated that this statement is related to the previous thought. He meant that if anyone lacks wisdom as to the explanation of trials and thus was lacking in maturity, he should ask God for enlightenment. Wisdom in the Bible is more than knowledge of facts. "The fear of the LORD is the beginning of wisdom..." (Prov. 9:10). True wisdom involves moral discernment, and this must begin with the knowledge of God, who has revealed His righteous standards. A further description of this wisdom is given by James in 3:17–18.

The source of wisdom that will enable a Christian to see beyond his struggle to the results God is achieving lies with God Himself. Every Christian is here encouraged to pray that such understanding may be given to him. An outstanding biblical example of one who prayed for wisdom is Solomon (1 Kings 3:9–12). If one needs encouragement to pray, let him realize that God gives "generously"

5. The noun cognate of this adjective is used in Acts 3:16 to describe a lame man who had been healed.

to those who ask for wisdom, and He does not "reproach" us for asking. It must not be imagined that these trials are punishments for sin, and if God is asked about them, He will reprimand even more. On the contrary, God wants us to pray to Him far more frequently than we do. The fact that trials have a way of driving us to prayer is one of their good results.

The thrilling promise to one who asks God for this wisdom is that "it will be given to him." There is spiritual discernment available, and God has promised to give it. Is this always so? How frequently one hears the complaint, "I asked God why, but received no answer." Reasons why this can be so are given in the following verses. However, it should also be noted that James did not state when the answer would be given, only that it would be. Sometimes not until much later does God reveal the reasons why He has allowed certain circumstances to enter our lives. Only then can the sufferer recognize what God has accomplished through the experience. The promise is clear: God will give the answer in His own way and at the time He chooses. The person who prays must be sensitive and patient.

VERSE 6. If this prayer for wisdom is to be effective, however, it must be made with trust, not with doubting. Failure here is one of the reasons why the answer may not come. When Christians pray that God will enable them to deal with trials in the proper way, they must have a faith that believes God is hearing and can answer. There must also be a trust (an element implicit in the biblical word "faith") that God's way is best, whatever it is. Arguing with God, complaining about circumstances, or hesitancy to be open to His answer are human attitudes that will prevent God from responding.

James's illustration of the doubting person who prays was the billowing of the sea, which is blown and tossed about by the wind. James had doubtless seen such occurrences on the sea of Galilee many times, for his boyhood home in Nazareth had not been far away. Even though that body of water is not large (fifteen miles long and six to eight miles wide), it was subject to frightful

Angry surf at Caesarea during a Mediterranean storm.

storms from the strong winds that sometimes funneled down to the lake in afternoon or evening from the mountains that rimmed it (see Matt. 8:23–27; 14:22–33). Perhaps James had upon occasion traveled to the Mediterranean coast and seen its surf pounding the shoreline, particularly during or after a storm.

To the author, the constant churning of the water suggested the agitation in a doubter's heart. Such persons are encouraged one moment, discouraged the next. It is interesting to note that the apostle Paul described spiritually immature children in similar terms, as ones continually deflected from a stable course by the battering winds of wrong doctrine, unworthy men, and deceitful schemes (Eph. 4:14). The man of faith is stable and mature. He may not possess all wisdom for every situation, but when he needs to ask, he does so in confidence that he has gone to the right source.

VERSE 7. That man, however, who goes through the motions of

prayer but has no real confidence that anything will happen, has deluded himself that an answer is even possible. On the contrary, James says he has no reason to think he will receive anything from the Lord. "Anything," of course, should not be pressed beyond its context. All men, including doubters who pray, are the recipients of countless gifts from God, although not from their praying. He provides sunshine and rain for the unrighteous as well as the righteous (Matt. 5:45) and sends fruitful seasons and joyful times for unbelievers as well as believers (Acts 14:17). James, however, was talking about receiving an answer to a prayer for wisdom to deal with trials. If a person has no real trust in God, it is doubtful that he would recognize any answer that came as being from God. More likely he would attribute it to natural causes or "good luck."

VERSE 8. The doubter's problem is that he is a "double-minded man."[6] He is doubting or hesitating between at least two ways of thinking. He has a divided allegiance, sometimes thinking God may help him and at other times abandoning that hope and finding no solution. He is unsettled, restless, vacillating.

The ramifications of this attitude are indicated by James when he says that a doubter is unstable in "all his ways." It is not just his prayer life that suffers. When a man has no stable understanding of God and thus no firm relationship with Him, he can have no truly satisfying philosophy of life. If one does not know that God is sovereign and controls all things and that He has made certain promises to His children in Scripture, adverse circumstances can be frightening indeed. A sense of hopelessness, despair, panic, or depression is often the result. Such a doubter tends to view himself as a victim of his circumstances, rather than a participant in the life and program of God, who controls our circumstances.

6. Grammatically no verb is expressed in this verse. The phrase "double-minded man" (*anēr dipsychos*) may be treated as in apposition with "that man" (*ho anthrōpos ekeinos*) of verse 7 (as in NASB), or as a predicate nominative after supplying a copula "he is" (as in NIV).

The mature Christian at such times is driven to God in prayer. He is encouraged to ask God and then trust Him for the answer that will come at the time God chooses. This was the experience and example seen in the early church (Acts 4:23–30). Sometimes, we must admit, trials seem to be the only way God can get us to talk to Him.

4. Both rich and poor Christians should glory in their spiritual position (1:9–11)

VERSE 9. The trials that believers encounter often cause a reassessment of life's real values. They frequently affect economic conditions and social standing. Rich believers can become poor, and the poor can become poorer. The occasion is offered for some careful evaluation of what is really important. James first encouraged the "brother of humble circumstances" to glory in his high position. Probably most of James's readers were economically poor. This would have been especially true during persecution, when material losses would be great. James himself came from a humble family (Luke 1:52; 2:7; 2:24, cf. Lev. 12:8).

VERSE 10. The sentence in the original Greek is elliptical, without a noun or a verb. English readers usually infer something like this: "But the rich [man/brother, let him glory] in his humiliation." There is little question but that the verbal phrase "let him glory" should be supplied as a parallel to the preceding clause. However, the identity of this rich person is debated. Some conclude that he must be an unbeliever.[7] It is pointed out that the rich are always dealt with severely in this Epistle (2:6; 5:1). Furthermore, it is argued that "pass away," and "fade away" in the

---

7. For example, Alfred Plummer, "The Epistle of James," *The Expositor's Bible,* ed. W. Robertson Nicoll (Grand Rapids, Eerdmans, repr. 1943), VI, 576; Henry Alford, *The New Testament for English Readers* (Chicago: Moody, repr. n.d.), pp. 1593–1594; Peter Davids, *The Epistle of James,* NIGTC (Grand Rapids: Eerdmans, 1982), pp. 76–77.

next verse, are not appropriate of Christians. It is also noted that if he were viewed as a Christian, the "humiliation" stated of him would seem to contradict similar terminology used with the poor man.

Nevertheless, the verse is more commonly interpreted of a wealthy Christian, for reasons that seem to be adequate.[8] Inasmuch as "brother" appears at the beginning of the sentence (v. 9), it is natural to infer its reference to both clauses. "Humiliation" would also be more difficult to understand if the man were not a Christian. To interpret it as referring disparagingly to his pagan wealth is surely strained and not quickly understood by the readers.

The best sense is to be found in treating the reference as describing a wealthy Christian (and there were some). He, too, could find reason to glory in his Christian faith, even in persecution. To be the object of ridicule and scorn because he had adopted Christian values would have been a humiliating experience for a rich man, perhaps even more so than for a poor one. To relegate material things to a lesser plane because the wealthy person had put his concentration on spiritual concerns would lower him in the eyes of many of his pagan neighbors. James said to him that this should be no cause for shame, but rather an opportunity for proper exultation that his values had now been straightened out.

When trials (including persecution) come to the rich man and threaten his possessions, he need not despair. Rather, he should recognize the temporal nature of wealth in comparison to the abiding values of spiritual life. Critics of this interpretation stress the fact that it is the rich man himself who is said to pass away, not just his riches. However, this statement by James was more likely a reference to all men, rich and poor. He was asserting that Christian rich men can have the right attitude toward wealth by

8. See Joseph B. Mayor, *The Epistle of St. James* (Grand Rapids: Zondervan, repr. 1954), pp. 45–46; James H. Ropes, *A Critical and Exegetical Commentary on the Epistle of St. James,* ICC (Edinburgh: T. & T. Clark, 1916), pp. 145–146.

realizing that all flesh (whether rich or poor) is temporal, and thus the physical and material life is not the supreme end (Isa. 40:6, Ps. 103:15; 1 Peter 1:24).

VERSE 11. James's description of the wealthy man and the comparative shortness of human life reminds him of the wild flowers that carpeted the hillsides of his native land. They were dazzlingly beautiful for a few brief weeks in the spring after the rains had come, but their beauty was always short-lived. Using poetic language that should have been familiar to his Jewish readers (Job 14:2; Ps. 102:11; 103:15–18; Isa. 40:6–8; cf. also 1 Peter 1: 24–25), James describes the scorching sun that soon followed the rainy season and withered the flowers that had sprung up. This was often accompanied by the blistering heat brought in by winds from the Syrian desert. The transitory nature of blossoms in Palestine made an apt illustration of the rich man (the poor man does not "bloom" with the display that the wealthy can have). When the heat of trials removes his flowering wealth, or threatens to do so, the Christian rich man knows that he would have it only a short time anyway, for he must pass away in due time just as every other man. Yet he has really lost nothing if Christ is everything to him.

5. He should look forward to the reward of successful testing (1:12)

"Blessed is the man" sounds similar to the Beatitudes, and there are other affinities to the Sermon on the Mount in this verse. However, the wording is not drawn precisely from Matthew's record. Here the man who is pronounced "blessed" is the one who remains steadfast under testing. This statement demonstrates that the previous discussion about the rich man was still on the theme of testing. It also shows that the trials in view have been outward ones that must be endured, rather than inward spiritual conflicts and enticements to sin that need to be resisted.

Those who remain steadfast in faith through their trials are promised the crown of life. This crown does not represent eternal life, for that is already possessed by every Christian (John 5:24; 1 John 5:11–12). It must refer, therefore, to one of the rewards for faithful serving, in this case the display of steadfastness under trial. It is called the crown of "life" because it is one of the benefits provided with eternal life.

Who has promised this crown? The early manuscripts vary at this point, some saying "the Lord promised" (presumably Jesus), others having "God promised," and still others simply "he promised." If it be assumed that the shortest and simplest is probably the original, it supplies the reason that the other readings arose to give clearer identification. Thus the text appearing in the most frequently used Greek Testaments gives the simple "he promised."[9] However, it seems obvious that the one who promised is either Christ or the Father. More specifically, Jesus did use such terminology at a later time to the church at Smyrna (Rev. 2:10). James may also have known of an otherwise unrecorded saying of Jesus. Of course, Jesus did promise a reward for those who are faithful under persecution: "Blessed are those who have been persecuted for the sake of righteousness. . . . Rejoice, and be glad, for your reward in heaven is great . . ." (Matt. 5:10–12).

Before Jesus left His followers, He told them, "In the world you have tribulation" (John 16:33). Paul taught his converts the same truth (Acts 14:22). James has instructed Christians how to respond.

Questions for Discussion

1. What are some good results of trials that have occurred in your life?
2. Can you name some instances in your life where God's answer to your prayer for wisdom came much later?

9. Nestle-Aland, 25th edition, 1963; UBS text, 2nd and 3rd editions, 1966, 1975.

3. What is the low position that a rich man should take pride in?
4. Why is doubtfulness in praying indicative of instability in other realms of life?
5. What is the crown of life?

3

Temptation—The Enticement from Within

James 1:13–18

The Christian life is not always the tranquil experience that is commonly expected. Believers are no less subject to trouble and calamity than are other people. They are often part of a minority, and this can provide special pressures. Their physical bodies are just as susceptible to disease or injury as their neighbors'. Their houses catch fire, their possessions are stolen, their jobs are lost, and their families are threatened—just like others'. These are the troubles that come from other people or outer circumstances. Some of them may arise because we are Christians in a hostile world. The Epistle of James addressed itself to this sober fact in the previous section (1:2–12) and explained how such occasions must be viewed as opportunities for God to mold His children into steadfast believers who trust God to see them through. The Christian can profit from such trials and should prepare himself to do so.

Another kind of trouble, however, is more subtle and is often more difficult to handle. This is the problem of evil thoughts, tendencies to sin, feelings of guilt and discouragement. In contrast to the previous discussion about the unpleasant things being done to us, the topic now shifts to those situations where we are enticed to do evil things. Every person has such temptations, and Christians are not immune. Some have tried to escape the problem by associating only with other Christians, or even by withdrawing totally from the world into some monastic setting. however, those who are perceptive and honest will admit that their sinful thoughts went right along with them.

James focuses his attention on this latter type of trial in 1:13–27. It is clear that he has shifted to a new topic, because the trials that come from without are to be considered "all joy" (v. 2), but the temptations described in the present passage are to be renounced and abandoned (v. 21). The matter is complicated by the fact that the Greek language James was using employed the same word to denote the whole concept of "testing"—whether outward troubles (i.e., trials, testing), or inward enticements (i.e., temptations). The reader must carefully follow the flow of thought to determine which aspect of the term is to be understood in any passage.

Even though the word family James used can convey either the good sense of testing or the bad sense of tempting, James may have given his readers an additional clue that he was shifting his discussion to a different aspect by the word forms he employed. In the earlier discussion he used noun forms only (*peirasmois,* v. 2; *peirasmon,* v. 12). When he talks about subjective temptation, however, he limits himself to verb forms (*peirazomenos, peirazomai, peirazei,* v. 13; *peirazetai,* v. 14). Furthermore, the discussion about testing also uses words denoting approval after the test (*dokimion,* v. 3; *dokimos,* v. 12). In contrast, the following passage intersperses such terms as "evil" (*kakōn,* v. 13), and "sin" (*hamartian,* v. 15), showing that enticement to evil is the aspect in view.

B. The Christian's Attitude Toward Temptation from Within (1:13–27)

1. The source of sinful temptation (1:13–16)

a) It does not come from God (1:13)

James begins with a prohibition against accusing God, because this is a frequent response of those who yield to temptation and then try to excuse themselves. Even though God is not usually blamed directly (more commonly men say, "The devil made me do it"), there are subtle ways in which the blame is shifted elsewhere, often to God. In the Garden of Eden, Adam excused himself for his disobedience to God by saying, "This woman whom Thou gavest to be with me, she gave me from the tree, and I ate" (Gen. 3:12). The frequently heard defense, "I'm only human," implies that the sinner could not help himself, and thus the blame is shifted to the Creator.

When James prohibited the excuse of "I am being tempted by God," he did not actually use the common word "by,"[1] which denotes a personal agent. Rather, he used another word that is usually translated "from"[2] and here points to a more remote cause. He meant that it is not enough merely to avoid blaming God for being the direct instigator of some temptation. We must not even imply that He is remotely responsible. God is not ever involved in enticing people to do evil.

The reasons why God cannot be the source of man's temptations are two. First, God's nature is untemptable by anything evil. He is absolutely holy; there are no weak points for temptation to gain a foothold. It is utterly unthinkable for the One who is

1. Greek: *hupo.*
2. Greek: *apo.*

inherently untemptable to be the cause of temptation in others. The second reason is God's activity. He never tempts anyone. God may test people (Gen. 22:1; Deut. 4:34; 7:19; 29:2; Ps. 95:8)[3] to strengthen their faith, but He never entices them to sin as this context is discussing.

b) It comes from within fallen man (1:14—15)

VERSE 14. The real source of blame for subjective temptation is not to be found outside of man but within him. James was not discussing how sin entered the human race in the Garden of Eden; nor was he denying the role of Satan in this matter. What he was explaining was how present-fallen man encounters temptation. Of course, it is sometimes the case that outward trials can themselves become the occasions for yielding to sin (for example, compromising one's faith to avoid persecution). James, however, was going to the heart of the matter in showing that the blameworthy aspect of temptation is inward, not outward. This was the teaching of Jesus in Mark 7:1–23.

"Each one" who encounters temptation is faced with the factors James described. He is tempted in the sense of being enticed to sin by his own desires. The term "desires" (*epithumias*) is more commonly translated "lusts" in the New Testament, although the Greek word itself was a neutral one. Whether the desires were to be understood as legitimate or sinful must be determined by the context. Here the sense clearly refers to desires that are aroused to do evil.

Two words describe the method by which a person's desires lead him into sin. The first one depicts the person as "carried away"

3. All of these references use the word "tempt" or "temptation" in the King James Version. More recent versions translate as "test" or "trial." The Hebrew word in these passages is a form of *massāh* or *nāsāh,* which in most contexts means to test the quality of someone or something, often through hardship or adversity. *Theological Wordbook of the Old Testament,* eds. R. Laird Harris, G. L. Archer, Jr., B. K. Waltke (Chicago: Moody, 1980), II, 581.

(NASB) or "drawn away" (KJV). The word appears only here in the New Testament, although another member of the word family occurs in Acts 21:30 and James 2:6 with the sense of "drag."[4] The second word, "enticed," comes from a root that means "bait."[5] It depicts something being lured to the bait and being caught. Combining both concepts and viewing them as metaphors of a fisherman, one can visualize the fish being first aroused from its original place of safety and repose, and then being lured to the bait that hides the fatal hook.

In similar fashion, every person has desires that seek gratification. All too often the desires are aroused and lured to seek their satisfaction in things that God has disapproved.

VERSE 15. The metaphor is now changed to a female who is impregnated and produces a child. The author does not attempt to give total imagery here, for no male is mentioned. Hence it was not the author's intention for his readers to attempt identification of the male who impregnates the female as Satan or something else (in this context the author is placing the source within the sinner, not outside). The sole point of the metaphor is to show what happens when desire is aroused and enticed.

"When lust has conceived, it gives birth to sin. . . ." The statement implies that sin occurs following the arousing of inner desires and the attraction to some tempting lure. Temptation *per se* is not sinful, for even Jesus was tempted (Matt. 4:1, Heb. 2:18).[6] To resist and flee from temptation is the appropriate response. Only when the temptation is yielded to is an act of sin committed.

Indulging temptation, however, yields an inevitable result. Just as a woman who permits herself to become impregnated will in

---

4. The term in James 1:13 is *exelkomenos*. The basic verb *elkō* without the prepositional prefix is employed in the other NT passages cited.

5. Greek: *deleazomenos*, from the root *delear*, "bait."

6. Although the unique joining of human and divine in Jesus prevented Him from yielding (God cannot do evil), it did not prohibit Him from being subjected to testing. The Bible specifically states that this was the case (Matt. 4:1; Luke 4:2).

due time produce an offspring, so desire that is gratified by enticement to evil has conceived something that will eventually reveal itself. The result will be sin—an act that departs from the way of righteousness and falls short of God's expectation. The term for sin used here (*hamartian*) is the most comprehensive term in the New Testament for moral wickedness. Consequently it is not possible to determine any particular type of sin James had in view. It is clear, however, that he was referring to the realm of sinful acts produced by indulged desires, rather than the sin principle within man, although it is fruitless to try restricting the reference to one specific type. He was speaking generically. All sin is the result of yielding to lustful desires.

Here the metaphor apparently is dropped, and the reality alone is discussed.[7] "The sin having reaching its full development" is a literal rendering of the Greek phrase. The use of the article "the" with "sin" makes it clear that James was referring to the sin just mentioned as the product of indulged desire. His point was that sin is not just an isolated act without consequences. There is a development that proceeds toward a goal. The root of the Greek term (*apotelesthesia*) conveys the idea of an end or aim. It is translated variously as "finish," "bring to completion," "run its course."[8]

The end result of sin is death. Its course is always downward. In the Garden of Eden, the warning was given regarding the tree of knowledge, and the sentence carried out: "... in the day that you eat from it you shall surely die" (Gen. 2:17). Spiritual death—the separation of man from God—occurred as the immediate conse-

---

7. Another view regards the metaphor as continuing and sees the birth of sin as being followed by a second generation in which sin grows to maturity and then gives birth to death—a stillborn or some abnormal birth. So A. T. Robertson, *Studies in the Epistle of James* (Nashville: Broadman, n.d.), p. 54. This is not as simple, however, as the view given above, inasmuch as death was most likely understood by James as the certain result of all lust, not as a distant or second-generation occurrence.

8. Arndt, p. 100.

quence of sin, and physical death followed eventually. James asserted that this principle is still true. Sin, if allowed to run its course unaltered by the redemptive grace of God in Christ, will bring eternal death. Physical death, still remaining as part of human experience because of the fall of man in the Garden (Gen. 3:19), will ultimately be overcome by the resurrection. In the meantime, physical death is not only the "last enemy" to be faced by every man (1 Cor. 15:26; Heb. 9:27), but at times it has been used as a discipline for sinning Christians (Acts 5:1–11; 1 Cor. 11:30).

c) *Christians must not be misled (1:16)*

The expression "Do not be deceived" is commonly used to call attention to some truth just spoken or to one about to be stated. Paul used it this way:

Do not be deceived [*mē planasthe*], God is not mocked . . . [Gal. 6:7].

Or do you not know that the unrighteous shall not inherit the kingdom of God? Do not be deceived [*mē planasthe*]; neither fornicators, nor idolaters, nor adulterers, nor effeminate, nor homosexuals, nor thieves, nor the covetous, nor drunkards, nor revilers, nor swindlers, shall inherit the kingdom of God [1 Cor. 6:9–10].

Do not be deceived [*mē planasthe*]: "Bad company corrupts good morals" [1 Cor. 15:33].

Jesus spoke similarly: "See to it that you be not misled [*blepete mē planēthēte*]; for many will come in My name, saying, 'I am He,' and, 'The time is at hand'; do not go after them" [Luke 21:8].

James used the statement in the midst of his discussion to stress the importance of his point that solicitation to do evil does not come from God. By placing it after the negative assertion and before the positive statement of what God *does* provide, the author has given an arresting appeal to his readers to realize the importance of what he was saying. It is thus a very effective transition to the next aspect of his thought.

The particular form of the command makes it possible to understand it: "Stop being deceived" or "Stop deceiving yourselves."[9] Given the universality of temptation and the natural propensity of man to shift blame away from himself, it would not be surprising to find James asking his readers to "stop" doing what all too frequently had been their practice. This command is no less valid for every modern reader. Our efforts to blame environment, poverty, bad luck, circumstances, or our humanness (which comes from God) have not enabled us to solve our sin problem. The reason is told to us by James: we have deceived ourselves by looking in the wrong direction. The root of the problem lies in the human heart and its desires, which seek satisfaction in wrongful ways.

By calling his readers "my beloved brethren," James softened any impression of harshness. He regarded them as true Christian brothers whose error in understanding had been more ignorant than willful. He hoped that his instruction would bring them more fully into line with God's truth.

2. The remedy for sinful temptation (1:17–18)

Although God is not the cause, He has done something about the problem. Rather than blame Him for man's predicament, the tempted should examine carefully that God has provided as the remedy.

a) God is the source of every good gift (1:17)

9. The use of the negative *mē* with the present imperative can denote a command to cease an action or habit already in progress. The form of this verb can indicate either middle or passive voice.

"Every good gift and every perfect gift is from above . . ." (KJV). The twofold use of the English word "gift" in the common version represents the translators' opinion that the two phrases are parallel not only in literary form but also in meaning. This is certainly possible, even though different Greek nouns are used, because each one can denote "gift." Nevertheless, understanding them in their more usual and distinctive uses yields good sense and is probably preferable. The first noun, *dosis,* uses a form that denotes an action—an act of giving. The noun in the second phrase, *dōrēma,* denotes what is given—a gift. "Every act of giving that is good" calls attention to the motive and purposes of the giver. "Every gift that is perfect" describes the gift that is appropriately suited to the person or the occasion. It is all that the gift should be. Therefore, in contrast to the evil enticements that proceed from within the heart of fallen man, good gifts come to us from above.

Such benefits come down to us in a steady stream[10] from "the Father of lights." This reference to God associates Him with the heavenly bodies—sun, moon, stars. This sort of terminology was not unfamiliar to James's Jewish readers:

> Then God said, "Let there be lights in the expanse of the heavens to separate the day from the night, and let them be for signs, and for seasons, and for days and years, and let them be for lights in the expanse of the heavens to give light on the earth"; and it was so. And God made the two great lights, the greater light to govern the day, and the lesser light to govern the night; He made the stars also [Gen. 1:14–16].

> To Him who made the great lights,
> For His lovingkindness is everlasting [Ps. 136:7].

10. The present participle, "descending" (*katabainon*), emphasizes the progressive nature of the action. In agreement with most commentators, it seems preferable to regard the participle not as part of a periphrastic with *estin* ("is descending") but as a further modifier of the subject. The literary cadence of the sentence is thereby enhanced.

> Thus says the LORD,
> Who gives the sun for light by day,
> And the fixed order of the moon and the stars for light by night
> [Jer. 31:35].

The benediction that preceded the recitation of the Shema in Jewish worship stated: "... Blessed be the Lord our God who hath formed the lights."[11] These heavenly bodies provided readily understood symbols of purity as well as constancy.

God, however, who made them is greater than they. He shows no variation or shadow caused by change. As constant as the heavenly bodies are, they do exhibit changes as man perceives them. Seasonal variations, eclipses, phases of the moon, clouded skies, and the shifting shadows seen hourly on a sundial—all were well-known instances of astral variations. But God's nature and character are unchanging. He does not shift from good giving to occasional evil giving. He never entices His children to do evil. All that He does is good.

b) God's greatest gift to man is regeneration (1:18)

By the exercise of God's sovereign will, He brought us forth into new life. It is clearly not God who brings about the deadly sequence of lust-sin-death. His will has made possible the very opposite. James has used the same word "brought forth" (*apekuēsen*) as in verse 15 to show the stark contrast between what God really does and that with which men have sometimes charged Him.

The statement is clearly referring to regeneration, the spiritual birth that is rooted in God's will and received by mankind through responding to the word of truth. This "word of truth" is the gospel, which tells of eternal life made available in Christ the Savior.

11. Alfred Edersheim, *Sketches of Jewish Social Life* (Grand Rapids: Eerdmans, repr. 1950), p. 269.

Palestinian figs, a common fruit in Bible lands *John J. Davis.*

God's purpose was to produce in believers a people whom James called "a kind of firstfruits" (NIV). Firstfruits are the first part of the crop, and are the intimation that a greater harvest will follow. In Jewish religious custom, the firstfruits belonged to the Lord in a special way (Lev. 23:9–10). James indicated that believers are the firstfruits "of his [God's] creatures" (KJV). If the expression is limited to mankind, the thought is simply that the generation of believers to whom James wrote was just a foretaste of a great host of Christians who would follow in future generations. However, the term *ktismatōn* is not in itself limited, and it is more commonly understood as "creation" or "created things." The New International Version has translated the phrase "firstfruits of all he created." If this is the proper sense, the meaning is that regenerated believers are regarded as the first stage of that ultimate renovation of all creation, which presently resides under the divine curse since the fall. Just as sin's stranglehold has already been broken for the Christian, and triumph over death is assured by resurrection, and ultimate glorification is guaranteed (Rom. 8:30), so removal of the curse upon the whole creation will someday be accomplished (Rom. 8:18–23).

There is a remedy for sinful temptation. Men must not excuse themselves and put the blame somewhere else. That will leave them as vulnerable as before. Rather, the sin-prone heart must be recognized, and then God's word of truth in the gospel must be heeded. By this means, God will bring us forth into new life where sin does not rule unbridled, and where glorious life, not death, is the prospect.

Questions for Discussion

1. What is the difference between the trials and the temptations in James 1?
2. Do you know of instances where sin brought not only spiritual death but physical death as well?
3. Is temptation always sinful? Explain.
4. How did God use "the word of truth" to give you new life?
5. In what sense are Christians firstfruits of God's creation?

4

Doers of the Word

James 1:19–27

The Word of God is crucial in man's quest for understanding himself and his world. In an age that continually confronts mankind with trouble, no merely human explanations or programs have been satisfying to any great degree. If man is ever to know how he fits into the cosmic scheme of things, he must look to God for explanations. James has explained that all men live in a world where outward circumstances are often difficult, and where inner pressures lead fallen men in paths contrary to God. Only if help comes from beyond man himself can he solve his problems of outward troubles and inward evil.

This is precisely what God has done by providing regeneration in Christ. The initiative was His, and the accomplishment was all due to His grace. The message has been announced to the world in the gospel, called by James "the word of truth" (1:18). God has done His part; now persons must respond to that word with acceptance or rejection.

One must not suppose, however, that James was advocating some sort of "bootstrap" program, whereby God's Word outlined a series of steps by which one could earn merit with God. He has already made it clear that it was God alone who "brought us forth" (1:18). It was His "gift" to men (1:17), and was the result of "the exercise of His will" (1:18). Man's responsibility is to accept or reject. The work of satisfying God's demands was achieved by Christ. It is His merits that God offers to us in the "word of truth" (see Rom. 3:21–24).

But what does it mean to receive the Word of God? The answer to that essential question lies in this section of James's Epistle.

3. The Christian's responsibility (1:19–27)

a) He must receive the Word of God (1:19–21)

VERSE 19. Although the truth stated here can easily be understood as a general principle, the words were written as part of a context. James clearly meant that every Christian must heed God's Word rather than his own ideas. There were problems in the churches in which some needed this particular instruction.

The manuscripts vary between *hōste* ("so that," followed by KJV) and *iste* ("you know this," accepted by most recent textual editors). The difference is only one letter in the Greek spelling and can easily be accounted for a scribal error. Assuming that the weight of documentary evidence supports *iste,* one confronts the problem that the word can be either imperative or indicative. If it was intended as an imperative, the sense here would be to "keep this in mind," "remember this." It can be noted that the vocative, "my beloved brothers," was preceded by an imperative in 1:16, and thus the literary structure would be paralleled here. If, however, the form was intended to be understood as indicative, James was saying, "You know," "I am not telling you anything new." This gives slightly better sense to the "but" (*de*) in the next clause. It is easier to understand the writer to add an adversative thought to his declaration ("you know this, but don't forget to do such and such") than to his command.

Four commands are given to explain what James meant. First, each reader should be "quick to hear." The mention of hearing rather than reading may reflect the usual way that the early Christians received God's Word. Most believers did not possess personal copies of the Scripture but were dependent on hearing it read at public services. The command called for an eager and prompt attention to the hearing of the Old Testament Scripture or the apostolic proclamation of Christ's teaching, which eventually became our written New Testament. Of course, one must also be open to hearing the Word of God as he is confronted with it through interaction with his Christian brothers.

Coupled with this admonition is the second one, "slow to speak." This was a caution against argumentation with the Scripture (or its proclaimer). There should be unhesitating obedience to the Word, not protracted discussion to circumvent it. The command also warns against promoting one's own ideas. There may have been a problem with the latter among James's readers (3:1–2). In this early time, when churches may have had considerable freedom for the members to speak in the assemblies, the unseemly rush to do too much speaking needed to be identified and prevented.

One should be "slow to anger." When eagerness to hear and heed God's Word is replaced by ambition to expound on one's own ideas, bitter arguments can soon develop. This is especially true when several in the congregation share the ambition to do the speaking. Those who are so certain they are right must be cautioned against wrathful argument. Of the various terms for anger and wrath, and one employed here is probably not denoting so much the passionate outburst as the persistent disposition of bitterness and dislike.[1]

VERSE 20. One reason why every Christian must be careful to avoid wrathful argument when he should be submitting himself to God's Word is that man's wrath does not achieve the righteousness of God. Defenders of God's truth do not further His cause by

1. TDNT indicates that *orgē* (1:19) is generally interchangeable with *thumos,* but it may contain an element of deliberation, which is absent from *thumos.* Gustav Stählin, "The Wrath of Man and the Wrath of God in the NT," TDNT, V, 419.

resorting to wrath, for man's wrath is usually mixed with other motives—ambition, revenge, jealousy, egotism, to name a few. Furthermore, men engaged in wrathful debate are rarely in possession of all the facts. Consequently man's speaking should always be done with an attitude of submission to God's Word—the final truth.

VERSE 21. The fourth command tells the readers to "receive the word implanted." The thought is combined with the negative aspect of removing everything that would hinder the accomplishment of this goal. "All filthiness" utilizes a noun that does not appear elsewhere in the New Testament, although the adjective form occurs in 2:2 as a description of "shabby" or "filthy" clothing.[2] "Abundance of wickedness" calls attention to the fact that sinfulness in men's lives is not only sordid in its nature, as the previous expression emphasized, but is also present in abundance. Christians must not become comfortable with their sinfulness but must face up to the fact that their Christian commitment allows no toleration of impurity in their lives.

"With meekness" (KJV) the Word of God must be received ("in humility," NASB). In contrast to the arrogance that a wrathful spirit denotes, the only proper Christian attitude is humble submission to God's revealed truth. When it is recognized, not just theoretically but actually in practice, that Scripture is God's unique communication with us; the implications of that truth will have far-reaching effects. When we recognize that God is speaking, we will want to be attentive, respectful, and in spiritual conformity to His wishes.

"Receive the word implanted" is a command addressed to James's Christian readers. They were his Christian brothers (2:1). He was not appealing to unbelievers to accept the gospel. The key to understanding his meaning lies in the descriptive "implanted" that characterizes "the word." He did not ask them to plant the Word of God in their hearts, for he has explained that God has

---

2. Another cognate, *rhupos* (meaning "dirt"), appears in 1 Peter 3:21.

already planted His Word in believers and has brought them forth to be His "first fruits" (1:18).

James was calling upon his readers to accept the demands upon their lives that the Word implanted at regeneration required. Perhaps James was recalling Jesus' parable of the sower, in which even the seed that fell on the good ground brought forth a wide variety of response (Matt. 13:8, 23). Those already born again into the family of God by accepting the gospel needed to continue using the Word to shape their lives and keep them from sin.

This "word of God" was able to save their souls. Obviously James did not believe in a salvation by works, but a salvation by the Word, which God has planted in their hearts. At the same time, his concept of salvation was not limited to the initial moment of regeneration, but it included all aspects of deliverance from sin into the light of full redemption. There are present and future aspects as well, and the Word of God has relevance to these also.

b) He must be a doer of the Word (1:22–25)

VERSE 22. The exhortation is given that believers must be "doers of the word." This was no new idea to any Jewish reader. Jesus had taught the same truth: "Blessed are those who hear the word of God, and observe it" (Luke 11:28). The Old Testament likewise expressed the importance of "doing" all that God's law required (Deut. 28:58; 29:29).

It is a subtle distinction, but well worth noting, that James wrote "be ye doers of the word" (KJV), rather than merely "do the word." This way of stating it places emphasis upon the kind of person the Christian is to be, not just some act he is to perform. One is reminded of the lawyer who questioned Jesus, asking "What shall I do to inherit eternal life?" (Luke 10:25). He was more concerned with finding out something to do than he was with being a doer. Later in his interview with Jesus, it came out clearly that he was more interested in finding out who his neighbor was than in being a neighbor (Luke 10:29). If he had truly been a neighbor, he would not have needed to ask the question.

James was clarifying the point that mere listening to the Word of God was not sufficient to fulfill the believer's obligation. It is possible to attend a worship service where the Scripture is read and suppose that one's responsibilities have all been met. The author was making the point that "hearers only" (KJV) were in no way entitled to congratulation. The term "hearer" has been found outside the New Testament of an attendant at a lecture but distinguished from a disciple.[3] It suggests, therefore, a more casual listener or auditor.

Unless the hearer of the Word responds with appropriate deeds, he is deceiving himself. He has deluded himself into thinking he has received the Word, when all he has done is let himself have a superficial encounter. A hearer who is not also a doer has usually deceived only himself. If his conduct does not match his Christian profession, his hypocrisy rarely fools his friends and neighbors, and it never deceives God.

VERSE 23. An illustration of the "hearer only" is given. A mirror in New Testament times was a piece of polished metal, usually brass, copper, tin, or silver, which gave an imperfect but serviceable image to the beholder. Many such mirrors have been found by archaeologists. The Old Testament laver for the tabernacle was made out of the metal from the mirrors of the Israelite women (Exod. 38:8). James here describes a person who looked at such a mirror to check on the appearance of his "natural face."[4]

VERSE 24. The "hearer only" is depicted as one who inspected his facial features in the mirror and then departed. The perfect tense of the verb "departed" (*apelēluthen*) implies that the depar-

3. J. B. Mayor, *The Epistle of St. James,* (Grand Rapids: Zondervan, repr. 1954), p. 70.
4. Literally, "the face of his birth or existence" (*to prosōpon tēs geneseōs autou*), surely used here with the sense of "his natural appearance." So Peter H. Davids, *The Epistle of James,* NIGTC (Grand Rapids: Eerdmans, 1982), p. 98.

Mirror and jewelry box from the Bar-Kokhba finds in Nahal Hever *Coll. Shrine of the Book, Israel Museum, Jerusalem.*

ture was a settled condition. He did not return to the mirror for a second look. It is going beyond the demands of the grammar to conclude that it was necessarily a hasty glance.[5] Whether the look at the mirror was long or short cannot be deduced from James's statement. What is clear is the fact that the departure became the settled condition. It was not followed by repeated inspections.

The departure from the mirror resulted in an immediate forgetfulness of what the mirror revealed. Since the look into the mirror produced no results, the episode was a complete waste of time and effort. It could have been dispensed with. The man whose look in the mirror reveals his tousled hair and stubbly chin but then fails to get busy with his comb and razor has received no benefit from the encounter. To James, the person who hears God's Word but does not heed it is just as ludicrous.

VERSE 25. James now describes the doer of the Word in contrast

5. Mayor, for example, paraphrases the thought: "Just a glance and he is off." *The Epistle of St. James*, p. 72

6. James Hope Moulton and George Milligan, *The Vocabulary of the Greek Testament* (Grand Rapids: Eerdmans, repr. 1972), p. 486.

to the hearer only. For the doer it was not superficial hearing but a concentrated attention. "Looks intently" translates a Greek verb that meant to look at something out of the normal line of vision (*parakupsas*). It is the same word used to describe Peter's stooping down to get a better look into the empty tomb (Luke 24:12), of John doing the same thing (John 20:11), and of angels who desire to investigate the glories of salvation that are outside their personal experience (1 Peter 1:12). One use of the term outside the New Testament describes a slave's craning his neck to catch a glimpse of some castanet players in the courtyard below.[6] Thus James was describing the doer as one who has such intense interest in the Word that he will go out of his way to study it (stooping or bending over its pages, perhaps).

That which has captured his attention is "the perfect law, the law of liberty." To what does James refer? The connection with verse 21 seems obvious. The "word implanted" is what saves believers, freeing them from enslavement to sin and condemnation.[7] Hence it brings liberty to its adherents. At the same time it can be called "law," not in the Mosaic sense of an outward code, but because it contains demands for compliance. James was referring to the gospel in its widest sense, called the "word of truth" in 1:18. Another reference is made to "the law of liberty" in 2:12.

To speak of God's Word as "law" is not to pit James against Paul, for Paul often used this sort of terminology. "Bear one another's burdens, and thus fulfill the law of Christ" (Gal. 6:2). "Where then is boasting? It is excluded. By what kind of law? Of works? No, but by a law of faith" (Rom. 3:27). "For the law of the Spirit of life in Christ Jesus has set you free from the law of sin and of death" (Rom. 8:2). This differs from the burdensome and

7. Bo Reicke states: "The freedom mentioned here is to be understood in connection with the remark in v. 21 that God's Word saves the souls of the believers. Thus the law of liberty is identical with the gospel of salvation, cf. 2:12." *The Epistles of James, Peter, and Jude* in The Anchor Bible series (Garden City: Doubleday, 1964), p. 23.

unsatisfactory aspect of the Mosaic law in that the compulsion for complying comes from within (Heb. 7:18–19; 8:6–13). Thus men are at liberty and at the same time can be obedient to God (see John 8:31–32). Hiebert stated it well: "Men are free when they want to do what they ought to do."[8]

The doer is also characterized by a continuation in his study of God's Word. "Abides by it" (NASB) or "continueth therein" (KJV) are renderings of the word that describes a remaining in the activity (*parameinas*). The doer gives it full attention and stays with it. He does not become forgetful, as described in 1:22–24, but follows through as a doer of the Word. He carries out the obligations that Scripture imposes upon him. Such a hearer is the sort James has been urging his readers to become. This is the only kind of hearing that is meaningful. To such James holds out the promise that they will experience the happy condition of spiritual blessedness that is the special joy of God's obedient children.

c) He must not be just "religious" (1:26–27)

VERSE 26. Having stressed the fact that receiving the Word of God means putting it into practice, not just hearing someone read it, James must still clarify one other factor. Being "an effectual doer" (v. 25) is capable of being misunderstood. Mere religious activity was not what James was advocating. Robertson commented: "Mere work may be perfunctory. One may be a worker only as well as a hearer only."[9] A characteristic of many people is their substitution of religious activity in place of a deeper spiritual commitment.

"If anyone thinks himself to be religious" is a preferable translation to the King James Version, which treats the verb as

8. D. Edmond Hiebert, *The Epistle of James* (Chicago: Moody, 1979), p. 137.

9. A. T. Robertson, *Studies in the Epistle of James* (Nashville: Broadman, rev. ed., n.d.), p. 71.

"seems."[10] Here is the case of a person who is deceiving his own heart by performing religious acts and supposing that this is what being a doer of the Word requires.

"Religious" (*thrēskos*) is a term that denotes the external acts of one's religious faith. In view here are such things as attending worship, observing the ordinances, reciting the creed, fasting, and praying. Every religious faith has its ceremonies and practices, and there is nothing necessarily inappropriate about them. Both Judaism and Christianity have religious acts that the followers are expected to perform. The danger appears when it is supposed that such performance entirely fulfills one's spiritual obligation. In James's illustration he cites the instance where a person performed these "religious" acts but did not keep his tongue under control. He was not "slow to speak" (1:19) and thus showed himself to be spiritually immature and probably incapable of mastering the rest of his body as well (3:2).

Instead of congratulating himself that he was truly a doer of the Word, such a man needs to know that he has deceived himself, and his outward acts are "worthless" (*mataios*). Whatever acts he was performing may not have been intrinsically evil and may even have been praiseworthy in certain respects, but if they were being relied upon as fulfilling his total obligation to obey the Word of God, they were useless for that purpose.

VERSE 27. James quickly acknowledges that true Christian faith does have its outward expression. There are externals to be observed that are "pure and undefiled" in the sight of God. He picks out examples from two categories, not to give an exhaustive definition of religion but to illustrate his point. First to be mentioned are examples of godly conduct in relationship to others. Sensitivity to orphans and widows in their emotional or economic distress was a frequent Old Testament exhortation

10. Although *dokeō* can mean either "think" (referring to one's own activity) or "seem" (as viewed by others), the context in 1:26 supports the former. He has deceived himself into wrong thinking. How he may seem to others is not the main issue here.

(Exod. 22:22; Deut. 10:18; Ps. 68:5). Since such persons were the most likely to be in distress in the ancient world, they provided immediate opportunity for the display of Christian love. One clear example can be found in the Jerusalem church during its earliest years (Acts 6:1–6).

A second realm in which to exemplify true religion is personal holiness and avoidance of spiritual contamination from the sinful world. "World" here is a reference to the world system with its values and practices, which are under the sway of Satan (John 14:30; 1 John 5:19). Careful attention to God's Word, followed by a conscious effort to obey its precepts, enables the believer to remain uncontaminated by the evil that surrounds him. This is true religion, not just religiosity.

Thus the passage closes with the theme declared at the beginning. Just as a genuine receiving of the implanted Word was shown to be incompatible with wickedness in 1:21, so conduct that is allowed to become stained by acceptance of worldly evils is inappropriate for a doer of the Word and reflects an erroneous notion of "religion" (1:26–27).

Questions for Discussion

1. Is it ever right for a Christian to be angry?
2. How does a Christian receive the "word implanted"?
3. What does "save" mean in 1:21?
4. What is the perfect law of liberty? What is the significance of each term in that description?
5. What is meant by being religious?
6. Should Christians be religious?

5

Favoritism—Breaking God's Royal Law

James 2:1–13

Discrimination is one of the great social tensions of our times. All sorts of people band together to exclude others from enjoying their special privileges. Sometimes the discrimination is based on race or color. Other instances reflect a favoritism arising from differences in religion, sex, age, wealth, or culture. Jim Crow laws, ghettos, and policies of certain clubs or neighborhood associations usually involve some kind of prejudice against persons who appear to be "different" from the rest. Even people's personal habits that seem offensive to others can trigger responses of discrimination and deny equality of opportunity or fairness of treatment.

Such unkind conduct may not be too surprising in a world where selfishness and the protection of one's own interests are the guiding principles. However, a higher standard is expected from those who profess the Christian faith. James has been asserting that proper religious faith has an outward demonstration. The Christian creed must be followed by Christian conduct. Furthermore, Christian conduct is not restricted to a few technical religious acts (for instance, baptism, communion, church atten-

dance) but also includes the display of godliness and love in every
aspect of life, as guided by the Word of God (1:26–27).

A recognition that Christian faith should make a difference in
the daily lives of believers is generally acknowledged, even by
those without any Christian commitment. Yet this very fact
provides its own problem. Some Christians do not exhibit the sort
of biblical conduct that is appropriate to their faith. The charge of
"too many hypocrites in the church" is frequently heard. When
Christian believers display the same defects of character as their
unbelieving neighbors, they bring themselves and their Lord
under suspicion and criticism.

The truth of the matter is that correction of many of these
conduct failures is neither instantaneous nor automatic. There
must be growth in the understanding of God's will for the lives of
His children. Consequently, in this Epistle, James addressed Christian readers about conduct problems they still needed to confront.
From the many situations in which sinful favoritism was hindering
their Christian testimony, the author chose the case of favoritism
toward the rich at the cost of mistreatment of the poor.

III. Favoritism (2:1–13)

A. The Exhortation to Avoid Favoritism (2:1)

By addressing the readers as "my brethren" and referring to
their faith in "our Lord Jesus Christ," James was clearly acknowledging the readers as Christians. All of the admonitions and
encouragements in the Epistle are based upon this assumption.

The grammatical construction in this command, "Do not hold
your faith . . . with an attitude of personal favoritism," utilizes the

present imperative verb with the negative word *mē*.[1] This usage commonly ordered the cessation of an action already in progress, and the understanding fits easily here, inasmuch as the readers were clearly accused of doing such things (2:6). Of course, the clause is also capable of being understood as "continually avoid the practice of...."

"Favoritism" or "partiality" is the more current rendering of the old King James Version term "respect of persons" (literally, "to receive a face").[2] The noun occurs in the New Testament four times, of which the other three all refer to God's absence of partiality in His dealings with men (Rom. 2:11; Eph. 6:9; Col. 3:25). A cognate is also used of God in Acts 10:34.[3] These precise words were not used in the Greek Old Testament, but the concept was found there.[4] The point being made by James was that Christians must not accept or reject persons on the basis of partiality, being impressed by position, wealth, looks, race, or any other superficial distinction. Such was explicitly forbidden by the Mosaic law, with particular reference to law courts (Deut. 1:17), but it is here made applicable to all situations.

Of special interest is the designation James gives to Christ, literally, "our Lord Jesus Christ the Glory." No matter how one finally interprets the last two words (i.e., *tēs doxēs*), this reference to Jesus by his half-brother is most remarkable. The post-resurrection

1. The view that the verb should be treated as an indicative used in a question encounters difficulty with the negative *mē*. If this were a question, *mē* would indicate an expected "No" answer, but this makes no sense inasmuch as the author knows that they do practice favoritism (2:6).

2. Greek: *prosōpolēmpsia*. The term is found only in Christian writers, and is obviously based upon the LXX expression *prosōpon lambanein*, which is a rendering of the Hebrew *nāsā pānim* (to accept a face).

3. Greek: *prosōpolēmptēs*.

4. The LXX uses the phrases *prosōpon lambanein* (Wisdom of Sirach 4:22; I Esdras 4:39) or *thaumazei prōsopon* (Deut. 10:17) or *epignōsei prosōpon* (Deut. 1:17) to denote unjust preference.

appearance to James must have been completely convincing as to
Jesus' full identity (1 Cor. 15:7).

The most common renderings of the phrase "the Glory" utilize
such translations as "the Lord of glory" as in 1 Corinthians 2:8
(by inserting a second "the Lord," or by adjusting the Greek word
order), or "our glorious Lord." The translation that requires the
least manipulation of the text regards the phrase as in apposition
to "our Lord Jesus Christ." Thus it is a further title, "the Glory,"
just as Christ is called elsewhere the Word, the Truth, the Life,
and the Light. That the Deity should be designated by the title
"the Glory" is clearly paralleled in 2 Peter 1:17: "... such an
utterance as this was made to Him by the Majestic Glory...."
Hebrews 1:3 described the divine Son as "the radiance of the
Glory" (literal). What is unusual is that James has taken a
well-known title for God and applied it to Jesus. A possible parallel
occurs in Psalm 85:9, where the Shekinah or Divine Glory may be
identified with Messiah.[5]

B. The Illustration from the Christian Assembly (2:2–4)

1. The case of a rich man and a poor man entering the assembly (2:2–3)

VERSE 2. James was writing a general letter to Jewish Christians
scattered over a wide area. Hence he was describing a supposed
case for illustration rather than a specific instance.

Even though the description is certainly of a Christian gather-
ing, the word "assembly" (*sunagōgēn*) was the regular term for
the Jewish synagogue. This is the only time in the New Testament
where the term is used of a Christian assembly. James himself
used the more common word "church" (*ekklēsias*) in 5:14.

5. J. B. Mayor, *The Epistle of St. James* (Grand Rapids: Zondervan, repr. 1954),
pp. 81–82.

A gold ring from Roman times *John J. Davis.*

Various explanations have been offered for this circumstance. Some suppose that the letter was written so early that Jews and Christians had not yet separated but were still worshiping together in the Jewish synagogue. An instance of this can be found at Ephesus, where Priscilla and Aquila remained in the synagogue after Paul's initial preaching of the gospel there (Acts 18:19, 24–26). On Paul's next visit he returned to that synagogue and continued his Christian ministry for an additional three months (Acts 19:1, 8). This seems to have been exceptional, however, and was hardly the pattern throughout the Diaspora.

It is more likely that among Jewish Christians in the earliest days of the Christian movement, the names "church" and "synagogue" were used interchangeably to describe the congregation of Christian believers. This would have been especially understandable among Jewish converts, who did not view their Christian faith as a repudiation but as the appropriate culmination of their ancestral faith. Numerous instances of this term to refer to Christian congregations can be cited from early Christian literature.[6]

These two men who are depicted as entering the assembly are apparently not regular attenders. Someone had to greet them and show them where to sit or stand. That visitors did attend Christian gatherings is clearly indicated elsewhere (1 Cor. 14:23). One of these visitors had visible evidence of great wealth (see the similar description of a rich father's treatment of his returned prodigal son in Luke 15:22). The other visitor was a poor man wearing shabby, dirty clothes, such as one might see frequently in that society of countless beggars.

Verse 3. The story then describes the assembly as looking upon the well-dressed person with special consideration and telling him to sit in a good place.[7] The poor man, however, is directed to stand, or else to sit on the floor by the speaker's footstool. (Obviously the speaker has a seat and is not offering it!) Clear discrimination was being practiced in the treatment of these two visitors.

2. The inconsistency of such favoritism (2:4)

James drives home his point with the rhetorical question: "Have you not made distinctions among yourselves?"—to which

6. See Arndt, pp. 790–791; Wolfgang Schrage, "Sunagoge," TDNT, VII, 840–841.

7. The Greek adverb *kalos*, "well," is regarded here as "finely, in a good manner, or in a good place." The suggestion of J. H. Ropes, based on his interpretation of

the expected answer was "Yes." The verb denotes making a judgment between two things, and the form used here (an aorist passive) usually meant to waver, doubt, be at odds with oneself.[8] James was confident that the very inconsistency of their action should have prompted doubts in their Christian conscience. By reacting to the situation as they did, had they not shown themselves to be judges with evil thoughts? If a judge in a court of law were to let his decision be swayed by superficial matters rather than by the essential facts of the case, it would be a gross miscarriage of justice. It is no less wrong for Christians to base their treatment of other human beings on such superficial matters as economic, social, or racial differences.

C. The Argument Against Favoritism (2:5–11)

1. It is inconsistent with God's action (2:5)

Using the address of a forceful and dramatic speaker, James urges his readers to listen to him as "my beloved brethren." Again he makes his point by the skillful use of questions, compelling the readers to think about the issue in order to make an answer. "Did not God choose the poor of this world?" The form of the question showed the expected answer to be "Yes." James was echoing the teaching of Jesus, which in turn had been drawn from Old Testament prophets. "He anointed me to preach the gospel to the poor" (Luke 4:18; cf. Luke 6:20; Matt. 11:5; Isa. 61:1). The poor "of this world" (*tōi kosmōi*) means "in the world's estimation, so far as the world is concerned."[9]

James did not mean that there was any merit in poverty, nor

---

an ambiguous phrase from Greek liturgies, that it should be rendered, "Sit here, please," has no clear lexical support, although it was adopted by RSV. *The Epistle of St. James,* ICC, p. 190.

8. Arndt, p. 184

9. Dative of reference.

that poverty was the cause of their election by God, nor that all the poor will be saved and none of the rich. He was merely recognizing that God had certainly not discriminated against the poor as a class. In fact, far more of the poor had responded to the gospel (viewed as the result of divine election) than had the rich and powerful (1 Cor. 1:26–29). This was so widely recognized that even in Judaism "the poor" was often a designation for "the pious." In the preaching of Jesus to his Jewish countrymen, He apparently equated "the poor" with "the poor in spirit" (Matt. 5:3; Luke 6:20). Of course, God has also chosen some of the rich; and furthermore not all of the poor put faith in Christ. But the general statement is clear and should be readily acknowledged.

"Rich in faith" is best understood as denoting the sphere of faith in which the riches of the poor exist. (James was probably not stating the content of their wealth as consisting of faith, but denoting the realm in which their riches are to be found, in contrast to the world where their poverty is viewed.) Those whom God elects are also constituted as heirs of the messianic kingdom, which He had promised through the prophets. James seems to view the kingdom in the fullest sense as still future (believers are the heirs of what is promised), even though there are anticipatory blessings to be experienced in the present. The words of Jesus were similar: "Blessed are you who are poor, for yours is the kingdom of God" (Luke 6:20).

The argument of James is clear: God has honored the poor, but the sort of favoritism some Christian readers were showing was in stark contrast to God's action.

2. It is inappropriate in view of men's actions (2:6–7)

a) The wealthy have been oppressing the Christians (2:6)

In the illustration James has given, the Christian assembly had dishonored the poor man by treating him shabbily in contrast to the deference they showed to the well-dressed visitor. Scripture commands believers to honor all men (1 Peter 2:17). James reminds his readers that their conduct was certainly strange in the light of the treatment they had received from many of their wealthy neighbors. He elicits their interaction with his letter by asking more questions. "Is it not the rich who oppress you and personally drag you into court?" In James's day, many of the rich and powerful were Sadducees, and they were the first persecutors of the Christians (Acts 4:1–17; 5:17–18, 26–40). Paul and Silas experienced similar treatment from some Gentile businessmen at Philippi (Acts 16:19). Jesus had predicted that His disciples would be taken before the courts of both Jews and Gentiles (Matt. 10:17–18).

b) The wealthy have been blaspheming the name with which Christians are identified (2:7)

By another question, James causes his readers to acknowledge that it was the rich as a class that had been the most powerful and effective opponents of the gospel, particularly in their vehement opposition to Christ. "The good name which has been called upon you" (literal) is based upon an Old Testament expression (Amos 9:12; cf. Num. 6:27; Deut. 28:10; 2 Chron. 7:14; Jer. 14:9; 15:16), which was also quoted by James in Acts 15:17. It described the believer as identifying himself with his God and henceforth being known as one of His followers. It is not certain whether James was referring to some specific time, such as baptism, when this may have been publicly performed (as some think), or was simply making a statement of general truth.

The name referred to is probably a reference to Jesus as Lord and Christ. The name "Christian" was not employed until around A.D. 47, just prior to Paul's first missionary journey (Acts 11:26), and this may have been later than the writing of James. The name "Christ" would not in all likelihood have been blasphemed, at least by Jews, because it simply means "Messiah," and this concept was not rejected by the Jews. It was the identification of Jesus as the divine Messiah that caused the blasphemy.

James was not denouncing wealth *per se* as evil. Neither was he advocating reverse discrimination, whereby the poor are to be favored at the expense of the rich. He was arguing against favoritism of any kind. At this point he was showing how logically and morally inappropriate his readers' particular kind of discrimination was. It may also be helpful to understand that James may have been using the term "the rich" with the same definition that Jesus did as "those who trust in riches" (Mark 10:24, KJV), not merely those who possess money.

3. It is a transgression of the royal law (2:8–11)

VERSE 8. "If, however, you are fulfilling the royal law." the words "if, however" (*ei mentoi*) suggest a slight modification of James's previous statement. He recognized that in the scope of this general letter, not everyone would be guilty of the favoritism just described. Surely there were some who showed kindness to rich visitors out of proper motives. Furthermore, James had not been teaching that rich visitors should be mistreated or discriminated against in favor of the poor.

The "law" in view here is obviously the law of God as found in the Scripture. The particular commandment involved, "You shall love your neighbor as yourself" is recorded in Leviticus 19:18, and was repeated by Jesus (Mark 12:31). It was a summarization of man's duty to his fellows and found in the second table of the law, which, of course, was derived from man's first duty to God (see Mark 12:29–30) as found in the first table. It is appropriate to recognize even the rich as one's neighbors and to fulfill the obligation of love toward them. Jesus wanted it clearly understood that he was not denying this truth.

James termed the law "royal" because it was the obligation of those who are "heirs of the kingdom" (2:5), and it emanates from the King. The description of the law as "royal" probably refers to the entire law (a deduction drawn from the anarthrous use of *nomos*), not just to the specific commandment from Leviticus 19:18.

VERSE 9. Partiality, however, which discriminates against one person in order to favor another, does not fulfill God's royal law. That was the issue to which James was speaking. Such action was sinful and was clearly a transgression of a specifically expressed standard in Scripture. Hence, God's Word has already categorized the perpetrators of such flagrant misconduct as transgressors of His royal law. It is totally inappropriate for the heirs of the kingdom.

VERSE 10. Sinning at even "one point" constitutes one as a lawbreaker. In the event that someone might excuse himself for what he regarded as a "small" sin of partiality to the rich, which would be outweighed if a conversion should occur, James denounces such thinking.

He constructs a hypothetical case of someone who kept the whole law, except for one instance. This case is purely theoretical, for James himself regarded all men as sinning more frequently than this (3:2). To sin even in one instance makes one guilty of breaking the whole law. He did not mean that such an instance means one has broken every regulation within the law, nor that when a person breaks one law it is then no worse to proceed to break others. His point was that God's law is a unity, being the expressed will of the one Lawgiver. Violating God's will at any point means that the offender has disobeyed God's intention. In any society, violation of a single law brings the law-enforcement system of the state into operation against the offender.

VERSE 11. A very simple and obvious illustration clinches the point. The same Lawgiver who prohibited adultery also prohibited murder. If one violates either of those ordinances, he is a transgressor of the law. The fact that a murderer may not have also committed adultery will not excuse him in a court of law. The keeping of some laws does not excuse a person for breaking others. One becomes a criminal by committing just one crime. So the sin of favoritism is not to be taken lightly nor excused on the basis of some ultimate good that might result.

D. Conclusion (2:12–13)

VERSE 12. James draws his discussion of favoritism to a conclusion by the solemn warning that Christians should always speak and act in view of coming judgment. The repetition of "so" (*houtōs*) does not look backward to the previous discussion but forward to "as" (*hōs*). The recognition that believers are about to be judged should motivate proper conduct toward other people.

Inasmuch as Christians are the ones being addressed, the literal "about to be judged" (*mellontes krinesthai*) must be a reference to the judgment seat of Christ, when believers' works will be judged (2 Cor. 5:10). James was not threatening his readers with the condemnation of the wicked but with the certain prospect that each Christian must one day stand before Christ and render an account of his obedience to his Lord (Cf. 1 Cor. 3:10–16). To the writer this event associated with Christ's coming could occur at any moment (*mellontes*, "about to be"), and thus it should provide an immediate and continuing incentive (see also 5:7–9).

At this judgment, believers will be examined by the "law of liberty." The law of liberty was first mentioned in 1:25, where it was clearly equated with "the word, implanted which is able to save your souls" (1:21). It refers to the Word of God as found in the gospel, together with its attendant obligations. This law of liberty sets believers free from guilt and from slavery to sin, but it also places them under the obligation to obey their Lord and Master. Christ holds His followers accountable not only for their faith but also for their works done in obedience. It is this truth to which James refers.

VERSE 13. Believers are reminded that mercy will be withheld from those who have displayed no mercy. Jesus taught this same truth. "Blessed are the merciful, for they shall receive mercy" (Matt. 5:7). "For if you forgive men for their transgressions, your heavenly Father will also forgive you. But if you do not forgive men, then your Father will not forgive your transgressions" (Matt. 6:14–15). "Do not judge lest you be judged. For in the way you judge, you will be judged; and by your standard of measure, it shall be measured to you" (Matt. 7:1–2).

James was not speaking of any final condemnation of true believers, but of the burning of unworthy works, which even a believer may experience (1 Cor. 3:15). God will not call evil good, whether it be in the realm of unjust favoritism or something else, and whether it be performed by a believer or a pagan. His mercy always operates in conformity to His righteousness. Christ bore the penalty for the believer's guilt in totality, so the matter of his justification before God is not in question. But each believer must still answer for his works done in the body, whether good or bad (2 Cor. 5:10), and rewards in heaven are affected thereby (1 Cor. 3:14–15).

"Mercy triumphs over judgment." With this triumphant exclamation, James ends his discussion on a thoroughly positive note. He was not advocating salvation by works. Rather, his viewpoint was the same as that of Jesus, who taught that a person will demonstrate his nature by his conduct. The Lord explained that acts of mercy are evidence of the possession of Christ, who produces this fruit in their lives (Matt. 25:34–40). On the other hand, the one displaying no such traits gives evidence that he has not been born again. At the judgment seat of Christ, only true believers will be present, so any absence of merciful acts must be occasional and not the unbroken pattern of that Christian's life. The believer, indwelt by the Spirit and developing the mind of Christ, should increasingly be exhibiting his new nature by acts of grace and mercy toward others. He then need have no fear of judgment.

Questions for Discussion

1. Is it always wrong to show special attention to someone?
2. In what ways do cultural differences compound the problem of sinful favoritism?
3. Was God unfair when He chose the poor?
4. If committing one sin makes a person guilty of all, is it no worse to commit many sins than a few? Explain.
5. What is the law of liberty? Why is it an appropriate name?

6

"Faith" That Is Dead

James 2:14–19

Faith is one of the great concepts of our Christian experience. "For by grace you have been saved through faith...." wrote the apostle Paul (Eph. 2:8). Yet some have pressed this to an extreme by implying that it makes no difference how one lives—faith is all that matters. Paul, however, taught no such doctrine. Although he insisted that people are saved through faith alone, he also taught, "Let him who steals steal no longer..." (Eph. 4:28).

The opposite extreme is that works are the way to win salvation. It has even been proposed that James supported this legalistic notion. Does he not say that Abraham was justified by works (2:21)?

To the superficial reader, it may appear that James and Paul hopelessly contradict each other. James clearly asserted that the Jews' illustrious ancestor Abraham was justified by works, and he then quoted Genesis 15:6 to establish his point (2:21–23). Paul, on the other hand, cited the very same passage and used it to conclude that Abraham was not justified by works but by faith (Rom. 4:2–5).

It should be observed, however, that both statements are true when it is understood what the writers were saying. They were discussing different kinds of works. Paul was explaining that performing works of law cannot make one righteous before God.

Only a genuine faith in God makes one acceptable to Him. James, on the other hand, was talking about the appropriate conduct that should flow out of genuine faith. His point was that a truly genuine faith in God will produce a changed life. Paul was in total agreement with this concept, for he wrote about "faith working through love" (Gal. 5:6).

To say it another way, James was addressing himself to the ever-present conflict between mere assent to a creed and a vital faith, which displays itself in action.

IV. Faith and Works (2:14–26)

A. *Faith Without Works Is Dead (2:14–19)*

The discussion begins by showing that a barren faith is really no faith at all. Perhaps James was confronting a Jewish-Christian phenomenon, which had reacted strongly to the emphasis on works in Judaism but had swung to the opposite extreme and was content with a mere profession of doctrinal orthodoxy. The author presents three reasons why faith without works is dead and therefore why such a position is false.

1. It brings no salvation to its possessor (2:14)

"What use is it?" asks James in this rhetorical question. The same expression occurs elsewhere in passages where the style suggests a dialogue (1 Cor. 15:32; see also Job 21:15). The answer expected is clearly that there is no use or profit whatsoever in the kind of situation he is about to describe.

A hypothetical case is envisioned in which someone claims to have genuine faith. Nothing in the context suggests that the person is attempting to deceive others. He claims to possess true faith, and one may assume that he was sincere about the claim. At the same time, however, this person does not display any works, which are the evidence that true faith exists.

James answered his first question by the response implied to his second question: "Can such faith save him?" (NIV). The Greek grammar makes it certain that the expected answer to this question was "No."[1] Thus the author has told us that a claim to possess faith is useless if no indications of life transformation are flowing from it. Furthermore, its uselessness is no small matter, for it pertains to the most crucial issue man can confront. Nothing less than salvation—man's acceptance with God—is at stake.

Confusion has been created in the understanding of this verse because of a poor translation in the King James Version. The translators ignored the presence of the Greek article with "faith" (hē pistis) and rendered the clause as "Can faith save him?" Inasmuch as the implied answer to the question is "No," the interpreter is immediately confronted with a contradiction, for Scripture is abundantly clear that salvation is received by faith. Hence James is sometimes pitted against Paul, and they are alleged to be advocating divergent means to salvation.

James, however, was quite careful in his wording. By using the article with "faith," he was making his reference very specific. He was not talking about faith in general, but about "the faith" which the person in his illustration was claiming to possess. Such translations as "Can that faith save him?" (NASB) or "Can such faith save him?" (NIV) are far better and represent the function of the article as particularizing the noun, perhaps pointing back to the contextual reference of the claim to faith mentioned in the preceding clause.

---

1. The use of *mē* with the interrogative verb shows that a negative answer was expected: "Such faith is not able to save him, is it?"

It should be pointed out that James was not arguing for two salvation requirements: faith plus works. He was not saying that some people have only arrived at the halfway point and now must add appropriate works to their faith. Neither was he contradicting Paul, as though Paul taught salvation by faith, and James taught salvation by works.

What James was contrasting was true faith, which inevitably produces action because it is alive, versus a mere claim to faith, which is profession only and has no life-changing power. Such a claim is spiritually dead; it is powerless to produce any works. It is not a faith that entrusts the soul to God's provision of grace in Christ.

2. It gives no help to others (2:15–16)

VERSE 15. Not only does a faith that is empty profession bring no salvation to its claimant, but it also offers no benefits to others. James illustrates his point by a supposed case of dire need,

Blind beggar in Jerusalem.

obviously calling for some demonstration of charity. The situation depicts a fellow Christian ("brother or sister") experiencing some of the most basic economic needs. Inasmuch as Christians bear a family relationship to each other as children of one spiritual Father, any genuine faith that has been effective in bringing about this new relationship would be expected to respond appropriately to the circumstances here described.

The term "naked" (*gumnoi*) can describe complete nudity, but it was also used of less extreme cases. The word could describe someone with no outer garment, without which no decent person appeared in public unless he was engaged in manual labor (John 21:7).[2] It was also used of persons badly clothed (Job 22:6, Isa. 58:7; Matt. 25:36–45).[3] Here it must be describing someone in desperate straits, whose clothing and food were not adequate, and who needed prompt and substantial assistance.

VERSE 16. In this supposed case, James continues by proposing that one of the readers might respond to the need of the brother or sister with a few pious words but absolutely no implementation of the assistance needed. "Go in peace" was the common Jewish farewell (Mark 5:34; Luke 7:50; 8:48; Acts 16:36). There is no indication that these words would be spoken sarcastically, but they do indicate that the encounter was over and that nothing further would be done to help the destitute person.

". . . be warmed and be filled." These verbs may be either middle voice ("get yourselves warmed and filled") or passive ("be warmed and filled"). A. T. Robertson suggests the middle voice as more natural here.[4] James H. Ropes, however, argues that New Testament Koine usage would have required the reflexive pronoun in addition to the verb in order to convey the idea "warm your-

2. Arndt, pp. 166–167.

3. Albrecht Oepke, "Gumnos," TDNT, I, 773–774.

4. A. T. Robertson, *Word Pictures in the New Testament* (New York: Harper, 1933), VI, 34–35.

selves." Hence he calls for the verbs to be treated as passives,[5] as do J. B. Mayor[6] and James B. Adamson.[7]

Favoring the passive idea is the fact that it was obviously impossible for the individual to "warm himself," and therefore a middle connotation would be insulting or sarcastic. Oesterley has suggested that the hypothetical speaker, who is one of the Christian readers ("one of you"), may have been evading personal responsibility by misapplying the words of Jesus, implying that the person in need should be trusting God for his necessities:[8]

> . . . do not be anxious for your life, as to what you shall eat, or what you shall drink; nor for your body, as to what you shall put on. Is not life more than food, and the body than clothing? . . . Do not be anxious then, saying, "What shall we eat?" or "What shall we drink?" or "With what shall we clothe ourselves?" For all these things the Gentiles eagerly seek; for your heavenly Father knows that you need all these things. But seek first His kingdom and His righteousness; and all these things shall be added to you" [Matt. 6:25, 31–33].

If such were the speaker's intention, it would be a gross distortion of our Lord's meaning. Jesus did instruct believers to trust God for their needs, but He also expected believers to share their goods with their needy brothers (Matt. 5:42).

It really makes little difference for the author's point whether the verbs are middle or passive. Either way the speaker was refusing to involve himself in assisting his needy fellows.

5. James Hardy Ropes, *The Epistle of St. James,* ICC (Edinburgh: T. & T. Clark, 1916), p. 207.

6. James B. Mayor, *The Epistle of St. James* (Grand Rapids: Zondervan, repr. 1954), pp. 97–98.

7. James B. Adamson, *The Epistle of James,* NICNT (Grand Rapids: Eerdmans, 1976), p. 123.

8. W. E. Oesterley, "The General Epistle of James," EGT (Grand Rapids: Eerdmans, repr. ed.), IV, 444.

If these pious words are expressed without accompanying acts of implementation, "What use is that?" James repeats the question with which he initiated verse 14. He meant that mere words in this situation are of no use at all. One is reminded of the frequent phrase, "The Lord bless you," which is equally hollow if deeds do not match the statement.

Scripture is not silent regarding the debt of concern that Christians owe to their fellow believers in need. From the very earliest days of the Jerusalem church, a plan was in effect to meet the needs of widows (Acts 6). When the plan became unwieldy, a new one was initiated. The apostle Paul instructed Timothy to teach the church at Ephesus that the needs of godly widows could not be overlooked (1 Tim. 5:3–16). The apostle John stated the principle with the utmost clarity: "But whoever has the world's goods, and beholds his brother in need and closes his heart against him, how does the love of God abide in him? Little children, let us not love with word or with tongue, but in deed and truth" (1 John 3:17–18).

3. It offers no evidence that it lives (2:17–19)

VERSE 17. Faith that is profession only can furnish no indication that it exists. It is a mere abstraction, a creed with no transforming power, a faith in name only.

In fact, James said it is "dead." There is no activity, no sign of life, no functioning beyond mere assertion.

The Greek phase *kath' heautēn* has been variously translated because its precise meaning is disputed. One method is to understand the meaning as "by itself"[9] and thus to render it as "being alone" (KJV) or "being by itself" (NASB). However, it is not clear that the phrase ever means this, and Ropes argues that such a

---

9. Peter H. Davids, *The Epistle of James,* NIGTC (Grand Rapids: Eerdmans, 1982), p. 122.

meaning would require the addition of the participle *ousa* (being).[10] The insertion of an additional word to produce sense is usually less convincing than other explanations that require no manipulation.

A better view treats the phrase as "in itself," that is, inwardly, or in its essence,[11] similar to several other New Testament uses (Acts 28:16; Rom. 14:22). The point would be that such a faith is not only outwardly unproductive but is also inwardly dead. It is not a matter of adding works to such a faith. It is rather the wrong kind of faith.

A third possibility should also be considered. A literal translation of the phrase is "according to itself." The preposition (*kata*) was often used to denote a norm or standard of measurement. In this instance, the sense would be that a faith that has no accompanying works is dead as measured by its own barrenness. "According to its own showing" is Lenski's apt rendering.[12] When one's claim to possess saving faith is measured by such an unproductive profession, it is shown to be lifeless. Such a faith may recite all of the correct words, but unless there has been a true commitment to Christ as one's Lord and Savior, it is powerless to save. It is like a corpse, which may have all the outward dimensions and configuration of a man, but if there is no evidence of life, the body is pronounced dead.

VERSE 18. At this point James introduces another speaker to enliven the discussion. "But someone will say" apparently identifies the speaker as an objector to what James has been saying. These words are similar to the expressions in Romans 9:19; 11:19, and 1 Corinthians 15:35, which clearly refer to an opponent. However, a problem is immediately faced because the objector seems to be saying that James insists on faith and the opponent advocates

10. Ropes, *The Epistle of St. James,* p. 208.

11. Ibid., p. 208; Oesterley, "The General Epistle of James," EGT, IV, 445; Mayor, *The Epistle of St. James,* p. 99; R.V.G. Tasker, *The General Epistle of James,* TNTC (Grand Rapids: Eerdmans, 1957), p. 64.

12. R.C.H. Lenski, *The Interpretation of the Epistle to the Hebrews and the Epistle of James* (Columbus: Wartburg, 1946), p. 579.

works, whereas just the opposite is the case. Many solutions have been proposed, none of which has been totally convincing. Fortunately the main point of James's argument continues to be clear: true faith will be energetic in displaying itself by its fruits, but a merely claimed faith without any observable effects is dead.

One interpretation of this passage regards the "someone" not as an opponent but as an ally of James.[13] The conjunction *alla* is treated as the emphatic "yea," rather than with its more common adversative use as "but." The sense would be that some Christian at random could say to an advocate of "faith only" that the difference between the two points of view is distinct, but the "faith only" person is unable to demonstrate that he has any trust in God. The entirety of verse 18 is understood as the speaker's statement. The greatest weakness of this view is its requiring the reader to understand "but one will say" as referring to a supporter of James, rather than to an objector. It is highly unlikely that any reader would have drawn this conclusion upon first reading the text.

Another view regards "you" and "I" as referring simply to "one" and "another." Thus the speaker is understood as saying that one Christian may claim the gift of faith and another the gift of performing good works.[14] He is saying that the two aspects can be divided and that presumably each position is legitimate. The latter part of verse 18 ("show me your faith...") is viewed as James's reply to this erroneous notion. This explanation has the advantage of regarding the speaker in a more natural way as an objector, but it falters in its insistence that "you" and "I" would have been readily understood as general references to "one" and "another."

Still another explanation regards the speaker as an objector but treats him as referring to someone of the readers as "you" and to James as "I."[15] The verse could then be paraphrased in this

13. Alexander Ross, *The Epistles of James and John* (Grand Rapids: Eerdmans, 1954), pp. 51–52.

14. R.V.G. Tasker, *The General Epistle of James*, p. 66.

15. Lenski, *James*, pp. 581–584.

fashion: "Someone who claims faith without works will probably object to this teaching and will say to some Jewish Christian, 'You have faith, which is really the important thing,' and he will say that I [James] am proclaiming a doctrine of works." This view preserves the adversative sense of *alla* (but) and construes the pronouns "you" and "I" with the appropriate concepts of faith and works. The chief weakness is the necessity of making "I" refer to James, whereas one would suppose that "I" in a direct quotation would refer to the speaker (i.e., the one objecting). Lenski answers this objection by pointing out that in this instance the employment of "he" (*autos*) would have introduced ambiguity, for it would not have been clear to the reader that the speaker was referring to James.[16] Consequently James has begun with a direct quotation and has concluded with an indirect one ("will say . . . that I have works").

Either of the last two explanations is preferable to the first, and this writer accepts the third as being most likely correct.

To the readers who have been wrestling with this issue and who have perhaps been attracted to the "faith only" concept, James hurls the challenge: "Show me your faith without the works, and I will show you my faith by my works." This statement is not part of the objector's comment, but is James's reply.[17] According to James, "faith only" is dead; there was nothing to show. On the other hand, he himself possessed true saving faith, which was active in producing Christian works of grace and mercy. He was not discounting faith but was proclaiming the fact that true faith is active, while mere profession has no life whatever.

Verse 19. James climaxes his teaching that "faith only" is useless for making us acceptable to God by drawing an analogy to demons. He points out the creedal orthodoxy of the readers and commends them for it. As Jewish Christians they had been

16. Ibid., p. 582.

17. niv has punctuated correctly by putting in quotation marks only the portion, "You have faith; I have deeds." nasb has included the remainder of verse 18 as part of the objector's speech.

accustomed to reciting their belief in the oneness of God through their regular use of the Shema: "Hear, O Israel! The Lord is our God, the Lord is One!" This formula, based on Deuteronomy 6:4, had been learned in childhood and was repeated morning and evening by every devout Jew. As Jewish Christians they may have continued using it after their conversion. Of course, this was not the total of orthodox belief, but it was one of the basic truths of their faith.

The readers are reminded that the faith that saves must be more than just intellectual assent to the truth, for even demons recognize this fact about God and yet do not possess the faith that saves. Jesus frequently encountered persons possessed by demons during His ministry, and they always recognized deity and spoke respectfully (Matt. 8:29; Mark 1:24; 5:7; Luke 8:28; Acts 16:17; 19:15). Yet it was clear that the intellectual understanding of God held by demons produced in them only the fear of certain doom, not the fruit of repentance toward God and trust in Jesus Christ.

The problem was not that their faith was insincere. On the contrary, they believed so completely in the coming doom that God has promised that they shuddered at the prospect. It is clear, therefore, that mere intellectual assent to the fact of God's oneness, as represented in the faithful reciting of the Shema, was not sufficient to save anyone. True faith must go beyond this to the point of trust and acceptance. It may be significant that the text does not use the regular constructions following the verb "believe" that occur in the New Testament to denote a saving faith.[18]

Barren faith is not simply a part of what man needs to save him. Such faith is dead. It is no more than empty claim or false profession. No good would be accomplished by adding works to

18. The verb *pisteuō* (believe) is regularly followed by the prepositions *eis, en,* or *epi,* or by the dative case alone in instances involving a genuine commitment to Christ. Here *pisteuō* is limited to a belief that God is one, without any hint of trust involved.

such a faith. What is needed is a different kind of faith—the kind that is alive and active. That faith will form the subject of the next section in James's letter.

Questions for Discussion

1. What is the difference between the works that James says are essential and those that Paul says are worthless?
2. What is true saving faith?
3. Can saving faith exist apart from works?
4. How does Christian faith differ from the faith that demons have?
5. What are some ways that you as a believer can demonstrate your faith by your works?

7

The Faith That Saves

James 2:20–26

The Christian church has provided sanctuary for some whose connections with it are merely external. To them the church differs little from a service club. Personal commitment to Christ is shallow, and the spiritual transformation that should follow is minimal, if not totally lacking. Consequently it is virtually impossible to distinguish them from the non-Christians with whom they mingle in the workaday world. It would doubtless come as a shock to their co-workers if they could see them in their places at church on Sunday. Of course, this rarely happens, because the two realms rarely overlap. Such "faith" is unadorned by any distinctive works. There is no visible connection between the creed that is professed and the everyday world where life is mostly lived.

On the other hand, some people let works take the place of faith. They may become so deeply involved in charitable works and social service that little attention is given to the development of a growing trust in God. In many cases, such works are not the demonstration of faith at all but are merely humanitarian impulses. They may be admirable pursuits, but they are not what James was discussing in his Epistle.

In the days of James, this problem sometimes took a different course. The earliest Christians came from Jewish communities. When they responded to the gospel and gave their allegiance to

Jesus as their Messiah, they learned that they were no longer obligated to the many works required by the Mosaic law. Christ had satisfied the law's demand, paid its penalty, and offered new life to all who would trust Him. Now the question was whether this freedom from the law meant that the followers of Christ had no responsibility to live righteously. Some Jewish converts apparently thought so, and they were being encouraged by unworthy teachers.

The burden of James's Epistle was to show that true faith is alive and active. Biblical faith is not just detached acceptance of an orthodox creed. Neither is it one-half of the requirement for salvation, the other half of which is works. James showed in 2:14–19 that faith without works is not true faith at all. It is dead, unable either to save its claimant or help anyone else. Rather than proclaiming a doctrine of faith plus works, James was arguing for a different kind of faith, a faith that is fully alive and shows its vitality by the things it does.

B. Faith That Works Is True Faith (2:20–26)

1. The probing question (2:20)

James continues his discussion with the hypothetical objector by raising a question that goes to the very heart of the issue, "But are you willing to recognize ... ?" The question was asking, "Do you really want a clear proof?" It was directed to the skeptical reader who may not yet have been convinced that intellectual assent to a series of propositions was not what God requires. That sort of "faith" was no more effective than what demons possess (v. 19).

More specifically, James intended to provide evidence that a so-called faith that is nonproductive of works is barren. A variant reading among the early Greek manuscripts occurs at this point.

One group of manuscripts has the word *nekra* (dead), and this was adopted by the KJV translators.[1] The word *argē* (barren, idle, useless) occurs in another group and has been generally preferred by textual critics.[2] A third variant *kenē* (empty) has been found in one early papyrus.[3] It seems probable that *argē* was the original term but was changed in some manuscripts to conform to the word *nekra* found in verses 17 and 26. If *nekra* had been the original term in verse 20, there would have been no reason for a copyist to suspect an error and to make the change. As for the variant *kenē* that appears in only one manuscript, it seems obviously to have been introduced by the nearness of the same term occurring seven words earlier in the Greek text.[4] Also favoring *argē* as the original word is the very possible play on words with the term immediately preceding. *Argē* comes from the same root (*erg-*) as the term *ergon* (works), with the alpha privative prefix negating it. Thus James was saying, "Faith without the works does not work." When used of horticulture, the word means barren, unproductive (2 Peter 1:8). It is used also of persons standing "idle" in the market place without performing any useful activity (Matt. 20:3, 6; cf. 1 Tim. 5:13).

"You foolish fellow" is literally "O empty man." It addresses the hostile (or at least unconvinced) reader as devoid of understanding on this crucial matter.

2. Two biblical illustrations (2:21–25)

James has clearly demonstrated that a faith without any works is not saving faith at all. Now he adds the final evidence by

---

1. *nekra* is found in Aleph A C^2 K P, and is the reading in the Byzantine texttype.

2. *argē* appears in B C* and among early manuscripts of the Latin, Coptic, and Armenian versions.

3. P^{74}

4. Bruce M. Metzger, *A Textual Commentary on the Greek New Testament* (London: United Bible societies, 1971), p. 681.

providing its opposite: that true faith works. Only that kind of faith ever receives God's verdict of righteousness.

a) Abraham (2:21–24)

VERSE 21. By going first to the example of Abraham, the author was appealing to a personage highly revered by Jews as their spiritual progenitor. It was Abraham who had been visited by God with a direct revelation to leave Mesopotamia and come to a land that would be given to him and his descendants. It was Abraham with whom God had made a covenant to bless with multiplied descendants, to form them into a great nation, and through whom all families of the earth would be blessed (Gen. 12:1–3). It was Abraham who believed in the Lord who had communicated with him and pronounced him righteous (Gen. 15:6). Any Jewish believer would have to be convinced that Christian teaching on this subject was consistent with the experience of Abraham if he were to adopt it wholeheartedly. At the same time, Gentile

Mosque of Abraham, built over the reputed burial place of Abraham at the Cave of Machpelah in Hebron.

believers as well were pointed to the example of Abraham, whose righteousness was received by faith (Rom. 4:9–12; Gal. 3:7–9). The expression "Abraham our Father" is sometimes used to demonstrate that a Jewish-Christian audience is in view.[5] Although it is certainly consistent with such an audience, the occurrence of the same designation in communications with Gentile readers limits the force of that conclusion.

James stated his proposition in the form of a question to which an affirmative answer was clearly expected as the appropriate response.[6] "Was not Abraham our father justified by works?" The plural "works" is a generalization, but the author had in mind one particular occasion—the sacrificing of Isaac by his father, Abraham. This event is described in Genesis 22:1–18.

It should be clear to the careful reader that James was not referring to Abraham's original experience of justification, which established his relationship with God, for that had occurred long before Isaac was born (Gen. 15:6). What the author was demonstrating was that Abraham's faith was not the sterile sort that was mere claim or intellectual assent. It was rather the kind that showed its vitality when confronted with the test. When his original faith showed itself by this stupendous deed, once again God declared His approval (Gen. 22:16 ff.).[7] Thus Abraham's works displayed the kind of faith he had.

The enormity of his faith in God must not be treated lightly. It was "Isaac his son" who was about to be killed by his father's hand. Is there not great poignancy in the very wording? Furthermore, he was not one of many sons, but that special son to whom the promises of God directly applied (Gen. 17:18–19) and whose

5. Donald W. Burdick, "James," EBC, (Grand Rapids: Zondervan, 1981), XII, 184.

6. The employment of *ouk,* not as a true negative but as indicating an affirmative answer expected to the question.

7. Although some interpreters have suggested that the verb "justified" is equivalent to "vindicated" here and has reference to the effect upon men who observed it, the context seems to point to God's approval, not man's.

birth had required supernatural intervention (Gen. 17:17; 18:11–14; 21:1–7). Any normal parent must stand in awe at the trust in God that characterized Abraham on that occasion. A more complete explanation of Abraham's understanding at that time is given in Hebrews 11:17–19. Knowing that God had obligated Himself to fulfill His covenant through Isaac, Abraham believed that God would resurrect his son, even though there had been no previous occurrence of this sort.

VERSE 22. "You see"[8] indicates that James still has his imaginary listener in mind. He asserts that the faith displayed by Abraham in the offering of Isaac "was working with his works." It was not a mental assent that was mere abstraction. The faith did not exist without results. The sort of faith with which Abraham secured righteousness from God in Genesis 15:6 produced the supreme evidence of its working in Genesis 22:1–16.

When James observed that Abraham's faith "was working with his works," it was obvious that he was not arguing for works alone. In fact, he was reflecting exactly the same understanding as Paul, who wrote about "faith working through love" (Gal. 5:6). But neither should it be supposed that faith and works are equal partners in the quest for righteousness. If James were viewed as teaching such equality, he would be in contradiction with Paul, who has taught clearly that faith alone saves (Eph. 2:8–9). James's point was that faith that saves is a faith that yields results. If there are no results, it was not real faith.

As a consequence of the works (*ek tōn ergōn*) that Abraham performed, specifically the sacrifice of Isaac, his faith was brought to completeness (*etelieōthē*). According to James, faith is not fully matured until it flowers into appropriate works. He did not mean that Abraham's faith was inadequate for justification before this

8. The verb *blepeis* is second person singular. Although it could be regarded as interrogative ("Do you see?"), it appears more probable that James assumes his statement would be agreed to.

act was done. If Abraham had died before the offering of Isaac, his genuine faith in God was fully sufficient to save him. Faith, however, is not a sterile, static thing but a living force that produces appropriate evidence as it grows.

It is faith that saves, whether it be that initial trust in God by the sinner or the more fully developed faith of the mature believer. The important feature is that it be genuine trust, not just mental assent. To illustrate, a maple tree is always that, whether it be in the form of the two-inch seedling that sprouts in the spring or the majestic leafy canopy spreading from a sturdy trunk. Yet it can properly be said that the tree has not been brought to completeness until it has developed through a full cycle and produced seeds of its own. It was nevertheless always a genuine maple tree from its earliest beginnings.[9] In like manner, Abraham's faith brought God's promise of justification long before he offered Isaac, but it came into full flower when he demonstrated its vitality during trial.

VERSE 23. By Abraham's great act of faith, "the Scripture was fulfilled." The reference quoted is Genesis 15:6 (a passage cited elsewhere in the New Testament in Rom. 4:3, 9, 22; Gal. 3:6). Thirty years prior to Abraham's offering of Isaac, he had believed the promise God had made regarding the magnitude of his descendants. At that time God noted his trust and declared him righteous because of his faith. God saw in Abraham the willingness to commit himself to an acceptance of God's will whatever the cost, and that attitude of faith met all the requirements for God's approval. It is because of this clear scriptural statement that believers even today rest their hope of salvation upon God's free gift received by faith.

But what kind of faith was this? Obviously it was neither an

9. This idea was suggested by J. B. Mayor: "As the tree is perfected by its fruits, so faith by its works." *The Epistle of St. James* (Grand Rapids: Zondervan, repr. 1954), p. 104.

isolated instance of mental assent to some fact nor an abstract or superficial acceptance of a religious creed. Rather it was the sort of dynamic and continuing trust that later made him willing to believe God and sacrifice his son Isaac when God commanded it, even though he knew that God's promise involved the descendants of the still-unmarried Isaac (Gen. 17:19–21). By successfully meeting this supreme test, Abraham's faith was brought to full maturity. Thus the Scripture that referred to an event much earlier was "fulfilled," for the reality and depth of his faith was demonstrated, and it was clear that Abraham truly had the kind of living faith that brings righteousness.

The mention that Abraham "was called the friend of God" is not a part of the quotation, nor is there evidence that God bestowed this accolade upon him because of his faithfulness in the Isaac episode. However, he was given this remarkable description elsewhere in the Old Testament (2 Chron. 20:7; Isa. 41:8). In fact, this designation for Abraham became so common among Arabs that to this day he is called El Khalil ("The Friend"), and their name for the city Hebron where Abraham lived and was buried is Khalil. Jesus gave this name to His disciples because He had made them His confidants by sharing His plans with them (John 15:15). Perhaps this is also the reason why God called Abraham "friend," for his faith was such that God was willing to grant him knowledge of His program for the future (Gen. 18:17; John 8:56).

VERSE 24. As James concludes his illustration from Abraham, he makes a statement that—if viewed in isolation from the context—seems in hopeless contradiction to Paul: "You see that a man is justified by works, and not by faith alone." However, James does not claim that works justify apart from faith. The previous verses clearly demonstrate this. P. H. Davids observes:

> . . . the two writers [Paul and James] are discussing totally different subjects. Paul is justifying the reception of Gentiles into the church without circumcision . . . whereas James is discussing the

106

problem of the failure of works of charity within the church (which may be totally Jewish).[10]

It is the "faith alone" notion that James refutes. Such faith is no true faith at all for it is barren (v. 20) and dead (v. 26).

Robert Johnstone has clarified the distinction by his illustration of a child's questions after a devastating thunderstorm. When the storm was over, the child asked a friend whether the damage was caused by the booming thunder that had stunned his ears or by the dazzling lightning whose brightness had shocked his vision. The answer was given that as terrifying as the noise of the thunder was, the destruction had been caused by the lightning alone, without the thunder. However, if an additional question were asked as to whether all lightning is the destructive kind, the answer would be "No," because destruction is not caused by the noiseless "summer lightning" that shimmers in the evening of a sultry day. Johnstone further explains:

Similarly, to him who asks, "Is it faith that justifies, or works?" Paul replies, "Faith alone justifies, without works." To him who, knowing and believing this, asks further, "But does *all* faith justify?" James answers, "Faith alone, without works, does *not* justify,"—for an inoperative faith is dead, powerless, unprofitable. Both statements, looked at in connection with the questions they are respectively meant to answer, are true, and both of vast importance. *Faith alone justifies, but not the faith which is alone.*[11]

10. Peter H. Davids, *The Epistle of James,* NIGTC, (Grand Rapids: Eerdmans, 1984), p. 131.

11. Robert Johnstone, *Lectures Exegetical and Practical on the Epistle of James* (Grand Rapids: Baker, repr. 1954), p. 224.

Jericho, the city of palm trees and home of Rahab.

b) Rahab (2:25)

The illustration of Rahab utilized a person who was in stark contrast to Abraham in virtually every way except as illustrative of an energetic faith. Rahab was a woman, a Gentile, a pagan, and a prostitute. Yet, by naming her, James was effectively making the point that the only faith that God accepts is a faith that works—whether from a respected Abraham or an unlikely Rahab.

Rahab was highly regarded by later Jewish writers. Traditions assert that she became the wife of Joshua and was one of the four chief beauties (along with Sarah, Abigail, and Esther).[12] The New Testament names her as a great example of faith (Heb. 11:31), and as an ancestress of Jesus (Matt. 1:5). The biblical references in

12. Mayor, *James*, p. 106.

Joshua, Hebrews, and James all designate her as "the harlot," and this fact should be admitted and not explained away. Efforts to render the term as "innkeeper" or "landlady" are without basis. Of course, Scripture does not condone her former life nor imply that she continued it after coming to faith.

The story of Rahab is recorded in Joshua 2. She was a Canaanite inhabitant of Jericho at the time of the invasion by Israel. She came to put her trust in the God of Israel after learning of His miraculous dealings with the Israelites during their wilderness wanderings (Josh. 2:10–11). Furthermore, she accepted the fact that God had given the land of Canaan to Israel (Josh. 2:9). James emphasized, however, that hers was not a mere passive intellectual recognition but a life-changing commitment. He assumes that she had faith, although he does not mention it (Hebrews 11:31 does state it), but he shows that her deeds proved the reality of her trust. When Joshua's two spies—here called "messengers" by James, perhaps because Rahab regarded them as true messengers from God—sought refuge in her house, she identified herself with the people of God. Instead of turning them away or summoning the authorities, she risked her life by hiding them. Then she fooled their pursuers by helping the spies escape through her house window, which was part of the city wall, and sending them west to the mountains where they would not be sought, rather than eastward to the Israelite camp. She had a faith that worked, and God obviously honored it by sparing her life and her family when Jericho was destroyed (Josh. 6:22–25).[13]

13. Rahab's lie to the agents of the king raises an ethical question, which James does not discuss (Josh. 2:4–5). Hebrews and James both attribute her hiding of the spies to her active faith (Heb. 11:31; James 2:25), but it is not necessary to conclude that her lie also arose from faith. *Lange's Commentary* calls her lie "a sin of weakness, which for her faith's sake was graciously forgiven her." "Joshua," *Commentary on the Holy Scriptures*, J. P. Lange, ed. (Grand Rapids: Zondervan, repr. ed.), p. 51.

3. The sober conclusion (2:26)

A simple but unassailable analogy ends James's discussion: "For just as the body without the spirit is dead, so also faith without works is dead." He looks at a living organism as possessing two indivisible elements: material (flesh, body) and immaterial (spirit, breath). To James the absence of the immaterial part from any organism was the clearest sort of evidence that physical death had occurred. Likewise any claim faith that does not issue in obedience to God is also dead. It is not true faith at all but only a spiritually dead intellectualism.

What James was explaining was the truth that biblical faith is a trust of the heart that actually obtains new birth from God. This new life cannot help but display its presence. He was neither pitting faith against works nor insisting on two things: faith plus works. Rather he was contrasting the true faith that works with a mere profession without any works. The first is genuine; the second is useless, empty, dead.

The teaching in James is not a New Testament innovation. Even Old Testament believers who genuinely trusted God performed deeds consistent with their faith. Doctrine and duty go together, for the one flows out of the other.

Questions for Discussion

1. Was Abraham's faith inadequate before he offered Isaac?
2. Are people justified by two things: faith and works?
3. In what ways were Abraham and Rahab similar in their faith?

4. What are some works in which you think Christians ought to be more actively engaged?
5. How involved should Christians become in the social problems of the day?

8

The Tongue

James 3:1–12

Communicating with words is one of the distinguishing marks of human life. It makes possible the clearest level of understanding, the conserving and transmission of knowledge from the past, and the sharing of thoughts between one intelligent being and another. By this means, God Himself has communicated with man, whether by the written words of Scripture or by His Son, who is the unique Word of God (John 1:1).

Like so many aspects of life that provide great advantages, however, communication through speech has its darker side. Sometimes speech can injure. It can do more harm than good. It can convey wrong information that can lead to disaster. It can be used irresponsibly, without concern for consequences. The solution is not to avoid it but to use it as God intended.

James recognized that his readers were experiencing difficulty in these matters. Considerable ferment and dissension were occurring in many churches. He indicated in this letter the need for more hearing of the Word of God and less talking about their own ideas (1:19). They needed to curb their unrestrained speech (1:26). Doubtless there had been much arguing over the issue of faith and works, some of which may have generated more heat than light (2:12). Speaking evil of others had characterized them far too much and had resulted in a judgmental spirit that was unworthy of their Christian profession. Some were actually placing their opinions above the Word of God and acting as if they had the right to judge which parts of God's revealed truth they could obey and which could be set aside (4:11). Their speech was getting them into trouble.

It was a natural transition for James to move from the topic of the wrong teaching on faith and works (2:14–26) to the heavy responsibility of the teacher who shapes the understanding of his followers. The primary medium they used was speech, but the possibilities for misuse were very real and exceedingly dangerous. Hence James proceeded to discuss teachers and the tongue, although the principles apply to every person. Verbal communication can either bless or wound; yet the Christian is responsible for living out his faith through works that flow from his regenerated life and bring blessing to others. Proper speech is a work that true faith must exhibit.

V. Teachers and the Tongue (3:1–18)

A. The Importance of the Tongue (3:1–5a)

1. The exhortation (3:1–2)

a) The command (3:1a)

The readers are told not to aspire to become a multitude of teachers. The author seems to be enlarging the theme introduced in 1:19. Perhaps there is a reflection here of the comparative ease with which nearly any Jewish man could gain an opportunity to speak in a local synagogue. Although lacking rabbinical training and authorization, Jesus had no difficulty receiving invitations to speak (Matt. 4:23; 9:35; 13:54; Luke 4:15–16). The same was true of Paul, even after he became a Christian (Acts 13:5, 14–15; 14:1; 17:1–2, 10–11, 17; 18:4, 19; 19:8). Perhaps there had been an abuse of this opportunity, not only in Jewish synagogues but in Christian assemblies as well. The tendency may have flourished because of the high regard for rabbis that existed in Judaism generally. When this was coupled with the natural human desire for prominence, it is not difficult to imagine a setting that called forth James's caution.

b) The reasons (3:1b–2)

VERSE 1b. Two reasons are given to justify the command just stated. The first is that teachers will incur greater judgment, presumably because they have greater influence and are thus more accountable. The word "judgment" (*krima*) does not always denote an adverse judgment, although it is most often used in an unfavorable sense.[1] James was surely not casting a negative reflection upon all teachers, for he includes himself in this very mention ("we shall incur..."). What he does assert is that to assume the role of teacher is a most serious undertaking because of its potential for directing the actions of others. If God is going to judge men for every idle word they speak (Matt. 12:36–37), how great is the responsibility of teachers, whose words are intended by them to be taken as directives for the lives of their hearers.

VERSE 2. A second reason for viewing the teacher's role most seriously is the fact that not only will he be judged more severely, but also no teacher is faultless. It may be questioned whether "we all stumble" is to be restricted to teachers, so as to mean "all we teachers stumble,"[2] or is a more general statement meaning "all

---

1. The KJV rendering, "condemnation," is thus unnecessarily harsh and misleading in this instance.

2. Bo Reicke, *The Epistle of James, Peter, and Jude* in The Anchor Bible series (Garden City: Doubleday, 1964), p. 37; James B. Adamson, *The Epistle of James,* NICNT (Grand Rapids: Eerdmans, 1976), p. 140.

we humans" or "all we Christians."[3] The commonest understanding regards it as a general reference to all persons or, more
particularly, all Christians, and this fits the thought well. Inasmuch as no one is beyond fault, and that includes teachers, then
no one is going to escape God's scrutiny. And if the scrutinizing of
the teacher will be even more exacting, one should not aspire to
such a role unless confident that he is properly prepared and is a
reliable instructor of God's truth.

The faculty of speech is then singled out for special emphasis.
Anyone who can master the use of his tongue, so as not to fall
into sin through angry words, misrepresentation, or falsehood,
shows himself to be a mature (*teleios*) man, having reached the
goal of full development. Inasmuch as the tongue is usually the
hardest member of the body to control, the ability to do so is
evidence of a pervasive maturity that speaks well for such a
person. Of course, the whole matter of maturity is a somewhat
relative concept. In the spiritual life there is always room for
further growth, and no one in this life reaches a state of sinlessness.
Nevertheless, Scripture does speak of a level of maturity that is
attainable and is expected of each believer (Phil. 3:15).

Although Reicke thinks that James refers to teachers as the
"tongue" and the entire congregation as the "body,"[4] it is more
consistent with the context to regard the "body" as the human
body or else as a metaphor for one's whole activity. Thus the
person who knows how to keep his speech under control reveals
that he has sufficient maturity to control his other activities also.
Oesterly suggests that the animated debates of Middle Eastern
debaters may be in view: "... the exaggerated gesticulations of an
Oriental in the excitement of debate is proverbial; that the

---

3. Peter H. Davids. *The Epistle of James,* NIGTC (Grand Rapids: Eerdmans,
1982), p. 137.

4. Reicke, *James,* p. 37.

reference here is to even more than this is also quite within the bounds of possiblity, cf. John 18:22; Acts 23:2, 3."[5]

2. The illustrations (3:3–5a)

James chose as illustrations two of the most obvious things guided or steered by man in that day, one a living creature and the other the largest man-made vehicle.[6]

a) The bits in the mouths of horses (3:3)

In both illustrations the analogy is between the small size of the controlling device and the much larger entity that it controls. In the case of the horse, however, the additional comparison may be that by controlling the mouth, one may control the whole creature. The application is obvious.

Although the horse was well known to James's readers, it was not an animal possessed by the average man.[7] The horse is first mentioned in Scripture in connection with Joseph's experience in Egypt (Gen. 47:17). In later centuries horses appear as the possession of kings and nobles and were used primarily for military purposes. The average reader of James would not have thought of a humble plow-horse but of a prancing war-horse, vigorous and high-spirited.

This most spirited of beasts, far larger than a man and with a

5. W. E. Oesterley, "The General Epistle of James," EGT (Grand Rapids: Eerdmans, repr. ed.), IV, 450.

6. Davids asserts that "horses and boats were the sum total of what men steered in those days," but this is claiming too much, taking no notice of the camel, the ox, or the donkey. *The Epistle of James*, p. 139.

7. G. S. Cansdale, "Horse," *The Zondervan Pictorial Encyclopedia of the Bible*, ed. Merrill C. Tenney (Grand Rapids: Zondervan, 1975), III, 204.

will of its own, could nevertheless be controlled through the use of a bit and bridle. This comparatively small instrument, when placed in the animal's mouth, enabled its master to control its movements and direction.

b) The rudder of large ships (3:4)

Turning next to the largest inanimate object that James's contemporaries might attempt to steer, the author mentions the great ships that plied the seas. Some of them were indeed very large. The Egyptian grain ship on which Paul was shipwrecked carried 276 passengers in addition to its cargo (Acts 27:37). Many of James's readers in the Diaspora must have seen such ships, and many may have sailed on them. Ships of smaller size were also to be seen on the sea of Galilee, not far from the author's boyhood home in Nazareth.

Inscriptions and wall paintings from antiquity have depicted numerous examples of large ships. The rudders resembled large paddles attached to the stern. Some ships apparently had two such rudders.[8]

Two factors are singled out by the author as making control of a ship difficult. One is its "great" size, and the other is the force of hostile winds. Yet, in spite of these adverse circumstances, the helmsman is able to exercise a measure of control by the comparatively small rudder.

c) The application (3:5a)

Just as the bit and the rudder are small objects in relation to the entities they control, so the tongue is a small member of the body, but it exercises a significance far out of proportion to its

8. E. M. Blaiklock. "Ships," *The Zondervan Pictorial Encyclopedia of the Bible,* ed. Merrill C. Tenney (Grand Rapids: Zondervan, 1975), V, 410–415.

size. It makes "great boasts" (NIV). And who can argue that the
power of effective speech is almost beyond calculation? Although
"boasting" is most commonly used in Scripture with a negative
connotation, that does not seem to be James's point here. He was
speaking of the tremendous influence of speech (whether good or
bad) in comparison to the small and unimpressive bodily member
from which it proceeds.

The author, of course, was not supposing that the tongue has
an independent personality in its own right, any more than the bit
guides the horse apart from the horseman or the rudder steers
the ship apart from the helmsman. He was using a common type
of Hebrew metaphor, just as Jesus did, whereby the bodily member is personified to represent the whole person (and particularly
the mind) who uses that member (Matt. 5:29–30).

B. The Dangers of the Tongue (3:5b–12)

1. It defiles the body (3:5b–6)

VERSE 5b. The reference to the great boasting of which the small
tongue is capable provided an easy transition to its negative
potential. Its possibility of creating great havoc is noted by Jesus:
"Behold, how great a forest is set aflame by such a small fire!" An
interesting play on words occurs in the original text with the word
hēlikos, which is used with both "forest" and "fire" with apparently opposite connotations. It can mean either "how great" or "how
small," and the context must determine the sense.[9] The word
itself denotes extremeness in size, whether large or small. A very
literal rendering would be, "Behold what-sized fire kindles what-
sized forest!" It takes just a spark to set a whole forest ablaze.

9. Arndt, p. 346.

James was doubtless familiar with such sights during the dry season in his homeland.

VERSE 6. The destructive effects of the tongue are now enumerated by describing the tongue as "a fire." Its capability of catastrophic destruction far outstrips its size.

Punctuation of this verse is difficult. In agreement with Mayor, the best sense is achieved by placing a period after "fire," and understanding "the world of unrighteousness" as a predicate complement with "is established" in the following sentence.[10] Thus the verse would read: "And the tongue is a fire. As the world of iniquity, the tongue is established among our members, which defiles the whole body. . . ."

To speak of the tongue as a fire was to use a well-known Old Testament concept (Ps. 120:3–4; Prov. 16:27; 26:21; Isa. 30:27). To identify it further as "the world of iniquity" is more obscure. Although the Vulgate regards the term "world" in the sense of "totality" or "sum," the use of the article—"*the* world" (*ho kosmos*)—makes a general reference to "a totality" less likely. It is hence preferable to interpret it in its frequent sense as "the present world system," regarded here as hostile to God and manifesting itself in our bodies by the tongue.

This present world system sets itself in opposition to God and is responsive to Satan (1 John 5:19). Fallen man shows himself to be a part of this evil system by using his tongue to express the evils that are in his mind, and these defile him (Matt. 15:10–20; Mark 7:15–23). His hatreds, impurities, slanders, and violent desires eventually find their way to the surface and are expressed by words. This use of the tongue "sets on fire the course of our life" (literally, "the wheel of the existence," depicting life as a continuing round of activity).

Nor is this dismal state to be viewed as simply an unfortunate characteristic of human life. James reminds his readers of the

10. J. B. Mayor, *The Epistle of St. James* (Grand Rapids: Zondervan, repr. ed.), p. 113.

eternal spiritual dimensions to this issue. Man's tongue, which gets him into so much trouble, "is set on fire by hell" (NASB). "Hell" is the Greek word *geenēs* (Gehenna). The term was drawn from the Valley of Hinnom, on the southwest side of Jerusalem. In Old Testament times the place was the site of Tophet, where the worship of Baal and Molech caused Israelites to sacrifice their children by fire (2 Chron. 28:3; 33:6). Josiah later defiled the place so no further idolatrous sacrifices could be offered there (2 Kings 23:10). Ultimately the site of the refuse dump for Jerusalem, its continuously burning fires provided the figure for eternal punishment, and its name—Gehenna—became a metaphor of hell, the place of eternal torment.

2. It is untamable by man (3:7–8)

VERSE 7. A second danger of the tongue is its inability to be brought under control by men. This is in contrast to men's well-known ability to subjugate all sorts of animate creatures, whether large or small.

The fourfold classification of creatures is the same as Genesis 9:2. The Greek text indicates a further grouping into two sets of two. "Beasts and birds" covers creatures that walk or fly; "reptiles and creatures of the sea" denotes those that creep or swim. It seems clear that James was attempting to include every kind of living creature.

The verb "tamed" occurs here twice in different tenses. The first is a present tense (*damazetai*) and asserts that this action is a present reality. The second occurrence (*dedamastai*) utilizes the perfect tense, implying that the present state is no innovation but has been existent from the past. The thought is that all of these creatures are presently subjugated by mankind and have been in this state from the past. The statement is a reminder of the mandate given in Genesis that man was to take control over creation (1:28).

It should not be insisted that "tamed" be understood in the sense of domesticated. The only other New Testament use of this verb refers to the subduing of a demon-possessed man (Mark 5:4). Hence the meaning is to subjugate, subdue, or control. Even though man has not been able to make a pet out of every wild beast or sea creature, he has been able to capture, cage, leash, or otherwise control any creature he wishes. Even the wildest of beasts can be put under man's control in a zoo. The reverse never occurs.

VERSE 8. This remarkable ability of man to control every other creature does not, however, extend to his own tongue. The literal statement is categorical—"the tongue no one is able to subdue" —with one significant qualifier. The very word order in the Greek text implies that the author had an exception in mind. A literal translation of the Greek word order yields this rendering: "But the tongue no one is able to subdue—of men." By placing "of men" by itself at the end, somewhat removed from "no one" (where it would be expected), the author appears to be implying that there *is* one who can control the tongue, but it is someone other than man. No one can subdue man's tongue except God. Of course, this does not imply that men's tongues are always out of control (just as wild animals are not constantly rampaging), but it does mean that man unaided does not have constant and permanent mastery of his tongue. It requires the supernatural power of God to subdue the tongue.

When the tongue is uncontrolled, it is "a restless evil and full of deadly poison."[11] Like a loose cannon, its danger is increased because one cannot predict where it will next unleash its venom. It can ruin character, break friendships, blacken reputations, and even send people to their graves.

11. No verb is expressed with these words. The phrases must be understood either as independent exclamations, predicate nominatives after the understood verb "it is," or as appositional with "tongue."

3. It acts inconsistently (3:9–12)

A third danger of the tongue is its potential for duplicity. Its inconsistent actions are set forth as contrary to the absolute standards of truth, which God Himself exemplifies and which are reflected in nature.

a) It is inconsistent toward God (3:9–10)

VERSE 9. Whenever Jews uttered the name of God, it was customary to add, "Blessed be He." In contrast to this exalted use of the tongue, however, humans also employ their tongues to call down curses upon other men. The inconsistency occurs because the very men who are being cursed are themselves made after the likeness of God. It is grossly inconsistent to pronounce blessings and praise upon God and then curse those who are patterned after His likeness.

The mention that men after the fall are still made in the likeness of God (Gen. 1:26; 9:6) reminds us that even though sin has marred the image of God in man, it has not been totally erased. Human life, therefore, is sacred, and every man to some extent still bears God's image.

James said "we" bless and curse, not because he was personally involved as an individual in cursing others, but because he was simply identifying himself generally with his readers, some of whom were doubtless guilty.

VERSE 10. The emphasis is upon the fact that the "same mouth" produces both blessing and cursing. The incongruity of the situation makes the speaker suspect. One aspect or the other must be false. Inasmuch as one whose heart is truly right toward God would not be guilty of vicious speech toward others, it must be the "blessing" that is hypocritical, not the cursing.

"My brethren, these things ought not to be this way." This kindly observation reveals that James clearly regards his readers

Salt-encrusted rocks on the shore of the Dead Sea.

as Christian brothers whose conduct needs some correcting, but who nevertheless are still part of the household of faith. Rather than a stern denunciation, the milder "these things ought not to be" would strike home to any sensitive heart with even more effect. He had already made his point. Inconsistency toward God raises questions even over the good things we have to say about Him.

b) It is contrary to nature (3:11–12)

VERSE 11. Turning to the realm of nature to illustrate his point that inconsistency is inherently wrong, James cites first a spring of water, which gushes from its opening in the rock with only one kind of water, either fresh (Greek: "sweet") or salty (Greek: "bitter"). The land of Israel is an arid country, where springs and streams are desperately needed and highly valued. Both freshwater springs and salt springs can be found, but two kinds of water do not flow out of the same opening. James states this as a question with the answer clearly expected to be "No." Nature itself does not deceive us with such inconsistency.

VERSE 12. From plant life James mentions three of the commonest agricultural products native to his part of the world—the fig tree, the olive, and the grapevine. The fig tree was such a common plant in Bible times that it was often used to picture the Jewish nation (Deut. 8:8; Num. 13:23; Hos. 9:10; Joel 1:7). Its first biblical mention occurs in Genesis 3:7, where Adam and Eve made garments for themselves with fig leaves.

The olive was also an ancient tree, mentioned first in the Bible in Genesis 8:11. Its ripe fruit was eaten, and its oil was used in cooking, medical therapy, religious ceremony, and as fuel for lamps. Wood from the tree was used for the doors and posts of the temple and for carved cherubim (1 Kings 6:23, 31, 33).

The grapevine has been cultivated in Palestine from earliest times. It was also used for a symbol of the nation, doubtless because the details of its cultivation were well known to all and provided apt analogies to God's care for His people (Isa. 5:1–7).

Each of these well-known plants produced according to its own nature. Fig trees did not yield olives, nor did grapevines produce figs. No duplicity or inconsistency was to be found. Hence James drew the conclusion that an objectionable source would not produce something pure: "Neither can salt water produce fresh." Perhaps James was thinking of that remarkable salt-water lake in his country, the Dead Sea, whose salt content was too great to sustain any kind of life.[12] Dead fish can be seen near the shore, after they have been swept into the Dead Sea from the fresh water of the Jordan River but very quickly died. I have seen freshwater springs with tiny fish in pools just a few meters from the Dead

12. The Dead Sea is referred to in the OT as *hē thalassa hē halukē* (the Salt Sea) in Num. 34:12; Deut. 3:17.

Sea, but those fish will die if they go with the stream into the salty sea.

The reader can draw his own application. An inconsistent tongue is contrary to nature. It indicates something wrong with the heart, which expresses itself by the tongue. With such inconsistency even the admirable things we might express from time to time are rendered suspicious because of the contradictory uses to which our tongues are often put.

Questions for Discussion

1. Was James trying to discourage Christians from becoming teachers? How does this fit with other biblical passages?
2. How is it possible for the human tongue to be brought under control?
3. Is the tongue the real problem, or does the cause lie deeper?
4. What are some types of problems you have experienced where an uncontrolled tongue created the difficulty?
5. Can you cite some examples where misuse of the tongue resulted in defilement of the whole body?

9

Wisdom—Natural or Heavenly?

James 3:13–18

The value of any message depends upon the truth and importance of its content. Yet for a message to be understood as "wise" implies some additional characteristics. Advice that is wise looks not only at the immediate situation but at future implications as well. Accuracy, practicality, both near and distant ramifications—these and many more factors must be taken into account before one's words deserve the designation of "wisdom."

What is wisdom? Is it more than just conformity to truth? Does it go beyond an abundance of facts? What is the difference between intellectual brilliance, impressive knowledge and recall of information, and the quality of wisdom that the Bible frequently extols?

The Epistle of James has been explaining the importance of responsible speech. Arguments among believers, angry exchanges, promotion of one's own notions without heeding the Word of God, and perhaps an unseemly rush to seize the public role of teacher in the church were examples of speaking that were not accomplishing the positive good for which speech was intended.

A theologian and educator of student ministers once said to an entering class, "To be a successful preacher the first requirement is to have something to say." He was emphasizing the crucial need for an accurate understanding of biblical truth. James has insisted upon this also, as he has taught that believers should be "quick to hear, slow to speak" (1:19). But there is an additional aspect to the wise proclamation of truth that James explains in the concluding verses of chapter 3.

In an era of specialization and emphasis on methods of effective communication, it is easy to ignore James's message. If the concentration is upon speech techniques, group dynamics, and motivational skills, the truth James was insisting upon can be overlooked.

As the reader considers James's words in their context, he recognizes that they have particular reference to would-be teachers in the Christian assembly. At the same time, however, everyone uses his tongue to speak and is a teacher in some way to those whom he influences. Hence the need to use the wisdom that is from above has relevance to every Christian.

C. The Proper Use of the Tongue (3:13–18)

1. It communicates wisdom (3:13)

Although this section of James is sometimes treated as a separate essay on wisdom, it is more likely that it is an integral part of the discussion on the tongue and its appropriate uses. It is the position of James that the function of speech is to communicate, and what is communicated ought to have worth. It should convey wisdom that merits the listener's attention. In this context he is focusing particularly upon the person who assumes the role of instructing others (3:1).

The wise and knowledgeable teacher reveals his wisdom through his conduct. By couching his words in a question, James implies that not everyone who tries to teach is necessarily qualified, and he calls upon each reader to examine himself in these matters. The principle set forth here is applicable to every Christian, not just to official teachers, for everyone uses his tongue to communicate, and what is stated should be reliable and helpful to those who hear, whether it be spoken in a church assembly, a classroom, or in private conversation.

"Wise" (*sophos*) includes the idea of knowledge above the average (so as to have something to teach). In this context it seems parallel to "teacher" (*didaskaloi,* 3:1), and our understanding should be influenced by this fact. It refers to the person who possesses "wisdom" (*sophia*) and can be a resource for instructing others. Every believer (not just official teachers) is supposed to be a wise person, exhibiting proper understanding of God's truth (Eph. 5:15).

The second description is "understanding" (*epistēmōn*). The term occurs only this once in the New Testament, but uses in the LXX and other literature establish its meaning. The word denotes one who is knowledgeable, skilled in some area of learning, expert. By combining the concepts of "wise and expert," James was referring to the person whose understanding was accurate and sufficient to enable him to be a reliable guide to others.

The assertion is here made that true wisdom and expertise will be displayed by the conduct[1] that is exercised. Mere knowledge is not enough, regardless of how extensive. In the Bible the wise man is not simply the person who knows the most. Not only facts but also attitudes are involved. The truly wise man is the conveyor of spiritual truth, and this must be exemplified by a godly life. "The fear of the LORD is the beginning of wisdom..." (Prov. 9:10; see also 1:7). Before one can begin to acquire the wisdom that can properly shape his own life and also help others, he must be in a right relationship with God. Only then can his mind be illuminated so as to be sensitive to God's truth and be freed from the spiritual darkness with which the fall has shackled him.

1. The Greek term *anastrophēs* is not adequately represented in modern English by the translation "conversation" (KJV). Although the thought of speech surely fits well in this context, the original term was much broader, including all aspects of behavior.

When a person has been transformed by the saving grace of God, his life will be changed. It should now be attractive (Greek: *kalēs,* good, beautiful). The products of his new life (Greek: "his works") will be the display of what has happened to his heart. This conduct should be performed "in the gentleness of wisdom." Gentleness (*prautēti*) is that quality that characterized Christ (Matt. 11:29). It is not passivity, or weakness, but strength under control. It is the opposite of arrogance, which demands that superiority be recognized (see v. 14). It is the humble recognition that even one's superiority in some area does not need to overstep the bounds of courtesy, considerateness, and kindness. Inasmuch as the wisdom discussed in this passage is not self-generated but is a gift from above (v. 17; also 1:5), a meek and gentle attitude is certainly appropriate in any teacher.

2. It may communicate earthly wisdom (3:14–16)

VERSE 14. All conduct is the display of a person's wisdom and understanding of himself and the circumstances. What we do and what we say are the result of what we think. Unfortunately not all "wisdom" is the proper kind.

James first points out the evidence of mere earthly wisdom among speakers. The presence of "bitter jealousy and selfish ambition" was a strong clue that something was terribly wrong. Apparently some in James's day were misusing their knowledge, letting it become the basis for self-glorification.

The phrase "bitter jealousy" (*zēlon pikron*) could also be rendered "harsh zeal."[2] Although the noun can be used in the good sense of ardor, zeal, or admirable jealousy, the descriptive "bitter" clearly points to a negative concept here. "Selfish ambition" is the proper translation of *eritheian,* as in all of its other New Testament uses.[3]

2. James Hardy Ropes, *A Critical and Exegetical Commentary on the Epistle of St. James,* ICC (Edinburgh: T.&T. Clark, 1916), p. 245.
3. Rom. 2:8; 2 Cor. 12:20; Gal. 5:20; Phil. 1:17; 2:3; Jas. 3:16.

The term is derived from a word family depicting the day laborer, one who worked for hire. It developed the negative sense of one who pursued only his own interests. This latter change in the sense reflects the scorn felt by the aristocratic Greek man of wealth and culture for the wage earner whose only thought was for personal profit.[4]

From these words it is apparent that the chief misuse of the tongue in view here was the rivalry and contentiousness among aspiring teachers. The bitter and fanatical zeal they felt for their wisdom, coupled with the selfish ambition by which they wanted to get ahead of others, led them to boastful claims of superiority. The same word was used by James in 2:13 of mercy "triumphing over" judgment. Here it speaks of the speaker arrogantly claiming to be victorious over someone else in his conveying of "wisdom," while at the same time displaying the very opposite of the meekness or gentleness that true wisdom possesses (v. 13).

Such boastfulness is to "lie against the truth," for it is contrary to the true wisdom of God. It does not represent the insight and truth that God supplies. He does not clothe His wisdom in such garb. James therefore commands the readers to abandon such preposterous tactics.

VERSE 15. The source and nature of such wisdom is next indicated. Stating it negatively first, James asserts that it is "not from above." Attitudes, explanations, denunciations, and plans of action that are accompanied by bitterness and jealousy are not indications of the kind of wisdom James has described in 1:5–8. God will give His wisdom to those who sincerely ask, but those who display the characteristics James has noted have not drawn upon that Source.

Positively stated, such wisdom has three characteristics. They are given in a climactic order, with the last one denoting the greatest opposition to God.

First, such wisdom is "earthly" (*epigeios*). This term does not

4. Friedrich Buchsel, "Eritheia," TDNT, II, 660–661.

of itself denote something evil. Jesus used it to characterize some of His teaching regarding mundane matters (John 3:12). Paul used it to distinguish a man's present physical body from the believer's future eternal body (2 Cor. 5:1). James uses the word to describe this wisdom as that which pertains to the earth and rises no higher. Its origin is earthly. Its motivations, methods, and aims are conditioned by what is temporal and mundane. Although it may exhibit much that is clever or expedient, it is restricted to earth even when discussing things pertaining to heaven. The concept picks up evil connotations from the fact that religious teachers are supposedly conveying truth whose origins are from heaven. The fact that it is strictly earthly wisdom is thus an inadequacy and a flaw. Paul spoke similarly of certain "enemies of the cross" who "set their minds on earthly things" (*ta epigeia,* Phil. 3:18–19).

Second, such wisdom is "natural" (NASB), "unspiritual" (NIV), or "sensual" (KJV). The original term (*psuchikē*) is not easily rendered into English. It belongs to the word family meaning "life" or "soul." The word was used by Jude of persons whose mind set was devoid of the Holy Spirit (Jude 19). Paul used the term to describe the unsaved man (i.e., the "natural man") who is incapable of understanding spiritual things, in contrast to the spiritual man (1 Cor. 2:14). He also used it of man's earthly, mortal body, in contrast to the resurrection body (1 Cor. 15:44). The common thread running through all of these uses is that the word describes what pertains to natural sensory life, not the product of God's transforming power manifested by the Holy Spirit as he regenerates man's spirit.

The final characteristic of this wisdom is its "demonic" source (*daimoniōdēs*). It is the result of promptings by evil spirits rather than God's Spirit. The ultimate source is not that insight into truth provided by illumination from the Spirit of God but the deception produced by agents of Satan.

The activity of demons is mentioned frequently in the Bible. Inasmuch as God desires to lead men by the influence of the Holy

Spirit, it should not be thought strange if Satan would attempt to counteract God's program by using evil spirits. Satan's temptation of Eve in the Garden led her to believe that taking his advice would make her wise (Gen. 3:5–6). Jesus explained during His ministry that certain false teachers were the spiritual sons of Satan and were carrying out his wishes (John 8:44). Paul revealed that certain forms of ascetic emphasis in the early church were the result of demons' doctrine (1 Tim. 4:1–5). John wrote that other spirits (i.e., false ones) beside the Holy Spirit can energize preachers and teachers (1 John 4:1–6). Satanic activity in the world may be much more frequent today than Christians commonly suppose. The concept of demonic influence should not be limited to pagan cultures nor the more extreme forms of spiritism. James tells us it is the source of much that passes for "wisdom."

Verse 16. The results of earthly wisdom are dismal indeed. Inasmuch as this wisdom is strictly human and does not have its origins or focus in heaven and in spiritual concerns, it is understandably vulnerable to the sinful tendencies that threaten all human enterprises. The presence of jealousy (or bitter zealousness) and selfish ambition in the heart, unchecked by the spiritual concerns that God's Spirit wishes to impart, prevents true wisdom from being exercised.

As a consequence, other things are almost sure to follow. "Confusion" (KJV) or "disorder" (NASB, NIV) are possible renderings for the noun *akatastasia*. Its commonest usage denoted political turmoil or revolution (Luke 21:9). It could also have the sense of personal unrest (Prov. 26:28). A more common New Testament usage refers to the destruction of the peace of a group by disputes or by disorderliness of conduct (1 Cor. 14:33; 2 Cor. 6:5; 12:20).[5] This last sense is the one employed by James. Instead of bringing enlightenment to the church through spiritual wisdom that comes from God, such a teacher brings only disturbance. He hinders

5. Albrecht Oepke, "Akatastasia," TDNT, III, 446.

rather than helps. All sorts of confusion, from public squabbles in the church to personal tensions and frustrations, are sure to result when Christians employ earthly wisdom. God is not a God of confusion (1 Cor. 14:33, same word), so it is clear that the "wisdom" being conveyed did not come from Him.

The introduction of confusion and disturbance into the congregation will also be followed by "every evil practice" (NIV). Wrong thinking produces wrong living. Hence confused thinking and faulty conduct are proofs that wrong wisdom has been operating.

It should be clear from James that the human intellect unaided by the Spirit of God is not a safe guide to spiritual truth. If left to its own devices, human wisdom very quickly can become tainted with sinful jealousy, personal ambition, and eventually with evil deeds. The fact that such can happen in the church makes this sad truth especially alarming. Even Christians (including leaders) can fall victim to human pride and ambition, and each one needs to be alert and sensitive to the possibilities mentioned here.

3. It should communicate heavenly wisdom (3:17–18)

VERSE 17. In contrast to the false wisdom of 3:15, there is a "wisdom from above," which our speech should always reflect. This is the wisdom that God gives (1:5), which has not only intellectual but also moral and spiritual qualities. It is a wisdom that is apparently available to every Christian who will ask God for it and be receptive to it. It is not dependent upon academic education or unusual intellect. Through the indwelling Holy Spirit, God will enable the humblest believer to walk in wisdom, displaying the characteristics here named. This wisdom is the understanding that sees things in their true relation to God's purposes and gives emphasis to spiritual and eternal issues.

Seven characteristics are given of this wisdom "from above," grouped into two categories. The first description, "pure" (_hagnē_), is set off from the others and describes the inner nature of true wisdom as free from defilement. The remaining six are introduced by "then" and depict the outward characteristics.

Heavenly wisdom is first "pure." This inherent quality governs everything else related to it. The Christian who is employing the wisdom from above will shrink from any thought, word, or action that is defiling. Christ Himself is pure (1 John 3:3), and obviously the wisdom from above will reflect the Source. Because this wisdom is inherently pure, no "doing evil that good may come" could ever be proper. How much finer Christian conduct would be if every action was planned only after first asking the question "Is it pure?"

From its basic character of purity come the six outward qualities. "Peaceable" (*eirēnikē*) describes heavenly wisdom as peace-making rather than strife-causing in its dealings with others. It will tend to settle disputes rather than provoke them. Man's tongue would be employed in ways opposite to what the user of earthly wisdom frequently does (3:8, 10, 14, 16).

The third characteristic is "gentle" (*epiekēs*), being considerate of others and making allowance for their feelings, weaknesses, and needs. Such qualities as being equitable, fair, reasonable, and forbearing are part of the rich connotation of this word.[6] It also contains the idea of not insisting on the letter of the law but showing a willingness to yield. It was commonly used of God, kings, or slavemasters who showed moderation or leniency to someone beneath them when it was actually within their power to insist upon their rights.[7]

"Reasonable" (NASB), "submissive" (NIV), or "easy to be intreated" (KJV) is the fourth characteristic. It explains heavenly wisdom as obedient or compliant (*eupeithēs*). In comparison with the previ-

6. W. E. Vine, *Expository Dictionary of New Testament Words* (Grand Rapids: Zondervan, repr. ed., 1981). pp. 144–145 (one volume edition).

7. Herbert Preisker, "Epieikes," TDNT, II, 588–590.

Cultivated fields in Jezreel Valley near Nazareth where James was reared.

ous term, which described someone in a superior position, this word depicts a subordinate in his relations with someone above him. Mayor reminds us that quarrels and rivalries in the church were undoubtedly due to faults among the latter as well as the former.[8]

Fifth, this wisdom is "full of mercy and good fruits." It abounds in the quality that is not only sensitive to the unfortunate but also actively gives aid to those who need it. In contrast to the evil works that result from earthly wisdom (v. 16), this wisdom produces good fruits by putting compassion into operation.

Sixth, it is "unwavering" (NASB) or "without partiality" (KJV). The term (*adiakritos*) describes someone who is not discriminatory, either objectively toward others or inwardly in the sense of doubting or being uncertain. Here it seems to describe avoidance of vacillation, whether in regard to the truth or toward persons. Such a person has clear discernment of God's will and thus can be

8. Joseph B. Mayor, *The Epistle of St. James* (Grand Rapids: Zondervan, repr. ed.), p. 132.

confident regarding the wisdom of his actions. He can walk a straight path without wavering from the truth.

The seventh characteristic of heavenly wisdom is "without hypocrisy" (*anupokritos*). It is open and forthright, without lying, deceit, or pretense. No schemes or subterfuges will form a part of this wisdom. Because it is a gift of God, it will be consistent with His character.

VERSE 18. The result of exercising heavenly wisdom is given in this concluding statement by James. He speaks of "fruit of righteousness" as being "sown." Although one commonly thinks of seed as being sown and fruit as being harvested,[9] James is already thinking about the crop that will ultimately be harvested. He has the viewpoint of a farmer who understands in the broader sense that he is actually sowing a crop when he plants his seed.

The expression "fruit of righteousness" is sometimes taken in the sense of "the fruit which righteousness produces."[10] This would be similar to the thought in Isaiah 32:17, where peace is stated to be the product of righteousness. However, it is just as likely that "righteousness" is a genitive of definition or apposition, so that the meaning is "the fruit which is righteousness."[11] This is the same thought that James has already expressed negatively in 1:20, where he said that man's anger does not produce God's righteousness. In 3:18 he seems to be saying that only peaceable speech (wisdom) produces righteousness. The latter interpretation seems preferable.

The achieving of this goal of righteousness requires that peacemakers ("those who make peace") plant the seed for that crop in an atmosphere of peace ("in peace"). By this action they are demonstrating their nature as children of God. "Blessed are the

9. NASB has supplied additional words to avoid misunderstanding: "And the seed whose fruit is righteousness is sown...."

10. D. Edmond Hiebert, *The Epistle of James* (Chicago: Moody, 1979), p. 237.

11. Peter H. Davids, *The Epistle of James,* NIGTC (Grand Rapids: Eerdmans, 1982), p. 155.

peacemakers: for they shall be called the children of God" (Matt. 5:9, κjv). By exerting their irenic influence through the use of heavenly wisdom, Christians may ease tensions, avoid strife, and encourage righteous living in others.

James, of course, was not urging peace at the expense of truth, for this could never receive God's verdict of approval (a necessary element of righteousness). What he was advocating was the exercise of a peacemaking spirit, which can bring an end to strife and bring all parties into conformity to the will of God. When believers use their tongues in this way, the problems James has described will be solved.

Questions for Discussion

1. What are some differences between the wisdom the Bible advocates and people's general understanding of the word?
2. Is it wrong to argue about Christian doctrine?
3. Is heavenly wisdom the automatic possession of every Christian?
4. Can you suggest instances from your knowledge where demonic influence was present in some form of earthly "wisdom"?
5. Can a Christian wise man always be at peace with others?

10

Worldliness—The Love God Hates

James 4:1–10

What we do results from what we are. Characteristics flow from character. Human actions are the product of the ruling principles that guide us. It is not true that we sometimes "act without thinking." Every action is the result of a decision. It may be a hasty decision or one prompted more by emotion than by reason, but in every case the mind has made a choice, which has then been pursued.

James has been describing these ruling principles as "wisdom" (3:13–18). He indicated that there are only two basic kinds of wisdom. One kind is "from above" and produces godly conduct, peaceable relations, and the display of spiritual virtues consistent with the Word of God. The other kind is limited to the natural world, is strongly influenced by evil forces, and produces arrogance, disorder, and impurity.

A careful reflection upon the Epistle of James reveals that the Christians of the first century were not much different from those of the present. Their lives were beset with problems from within and without. They had difficulty in relating properly to others, especially those from another economic class. Some of them wondered how Christian works fit into the format of salvation by grace through faith. Many were talking too much—arguing, criticizing, pushing themselves forward. Their tongues were getting them into trouble. They were exhibiting the kind of wisdom that was operating within them.

As Christians today assess their lives, there are some questions to be asked that may help identify the ruling principle behind their actions. What activities do we tend to emphasize? What matters upset us most easily? When crisis comes, what factors take precedence? In unpleasant situations, does our personal contribution tend to pacify or to cause strife? Do we take offense easily if our ideas are not followed, or do we frequently defer to others? All of our actions stem from the wisdom we employ, and the symptoms for accurate diagnosis are readily apparent. James was not willing, however, merely to name the two kinds of wisdom. He went on to elaborate why the wisdom from above is not universally utilized by Christians. He explained that there are hindrances to the employment of spiritual wisdom, and the chief hindrance lies within ourselves, not outside. To that issue the next portion of James's Epistle is addressed.

VI. Worldliness and Strife (4:1–7)

Worldliness is a concept that is commonly viewed in a different fashion by present-day Christians. All too frequently worldliness is thought of in terms of a list of taboos that every serious Christian should avoid. James, however, approaches the matter differently. Questionable practices are the symptoms. James focuses on the disease.

A. The Problem (4:1–5)

1. Wars and fightings (4:1–3)

VERSE 1. Instead of the peace that should characterize Christian relations (3:18), all too often there are wars and fightings. Although James uses the terminology of warfare, the mention of "among you" makes it clear that he was not referring to international conflict but rather to strife among Christians in their gatherings and their personal contacts. "Wars" (*polemoi*) refers to the general state of hostility that may include many "battles" (*machai*). The latter word refers to specific outbursts of the conflict. James is thus depicting situations in which occasions of disagreement result in continuing hostility, even after the battle is over. Armed camps develop, and true peace is not achieved.

James is not content to concentrate on the strife; he compels his readers to think about the cause. Twice he uses the word *pothen* (whence?, from where?) to emphasize this feature.[1] A literal rendering of the question would be this: "From where [come] wars and from where [come] battles among you?" He then answers the question with another: "[Do they not come] from here—from your pleasures which are waging war in your members?"

The term "pleasures" (NASB) or "desires" (NIV) translates the word *hēdonē*, reflected in our English term "hedonism." It is used consistently in the New Testament of sinful pleasures or the desire for them.[2] James uses the word to describe the sinful desire for satisfaction, which is self-seeking and causes those who yield to it to wrangle with one another in order to get their own way.

It is further explained that these yearnings for pleasurable

---

1. KJV follows the Textus Receptus, which uses *pothen* only once. Manuscript evidence, however, is very strong for the double use.
2. Other NT uses are Luke 8:14; Titus 3:3; James 4:3; 2 Peter 2:13.

gratifications are constantly waging war among Christians by using the varous members of our bodies. The sin principle has been dethroned from its mastery of the regenerated human spirit, but it continues to make its presence felt through the yearnings of our minds and bodies—whether it be the sexual drive, desire for material possessions, yearnings for dominance, or as previously mentioned by James, the misuse of the tongue. Paul wrote similarly: "For I joyfully concur with the law of God in the inner man, but I see a different law in the members of my body, waging war against the law of my mind, and making me a prisoner of the law of sin which is in my members" (Rom. 7:22–23). Sin, of course, is essentially a spiritual problem and merely utilizes the physical body as its instrument.

VERSE 2. The problem was that the readers were descending to the wisdom of the world and were not asking God for His wisdom. When their cravings for satisfaction were not being met, they resorted to sinful means to acquire it or to seek revenge.

Two problems confront the interpreter in this verse. One has to do with the punctuation of the clauses; the other concerns the meaning of "kill." As the text is translated in the King James and New International versions, a rather strange anticlimax results. "Ye kill, and desire to have, and cannot obtain" (KJV). The New International is equally awkward: "You kill and covet, but you cannot have what you want." Inasmuch as the earliest manuscripts had no punctuation at all, the translator must make such decisions himself. Many have adopted the punctuation offered in the Nestle-Aland, the UBS Greek text, and supported by such commentators as Mayor[3] and Ropes.[4] This punctuation appears in the text of numerous modern versions, such as the Revised Standard and the New American Standard. It avoids the anti-

3. J. B. Mayor, *The Epistle of James* (Grand Rapids: Zondervan, 1913 repr.), pp. 135–137.

4. James Ropes, *A Critical and Exegetical Commentary on the Epistle of St. James*, ICC (Edinburgh: T. & T. Clark, 1916), p. 254.

climax by punctuating as follows: "You lust and do not have; [so] you kill. And you covet and are not able to obtain; [so] you fight and wage war." The awkwardness, however, is now transferred to the need to supply a conjunction such as "so." Furthermore, the presence of the unneeded "and" (*kai*) before "you covet" is also awkward and has been so noted.[5]

The second problem concerns the meaning of "you kill" (*phoneuete*). Is it literal or metaphorical? In the sixteenth century, Erasmus saw the anticlimax problem and conjectured that the proper reading should be "you envy" (*pthoneite*), a word similar in appearance. Unfortunately for this possibility, it is without any manuscript support. Those who regard "kill" as literal here view it as stating the final outcome of such a course of action.[6] However, it seems more likely that "kill" is figurative, referring to anger and hatred in the same manner as Jesus did (Matt. 5:21–22; see also 1 John 3:15). This would be appropriate in this context, where the term "wars and battles" is surely metaphorical. Furthermore, if it were literal, we must suppose that actual Christian murderers were present in these congregations, whereas Roman justice would have intervened in such cases. Finally, to understand it as a metaphor for hatred removes much of the force from the charge of rhetorical anticlimax and allows the punctuation to be left as it has traditionally been.

The problem of many Christians in dealing with the desires for gratification that everyone possesses is that God's wisdom is not actively sought. The right things are not asked for, God's point of view revealed in Scripture has not been understood, and there is often little sensitivity to the answer God longs to give.

VERSE 3. James has just said that his readers did not have what they desired because they did not ask. Now he says that they did ask, but they did not receive because their asking was improper.

---

5. Peter H. Davids, *The Epistle of James*, NIGTC (Grand Rapids: Eerdmans, 1982), p. 158.

6. For example, J. Ropes, *James*, pp. 254–255.

Apparently the first statement was not meant to imply that they did not ask at all. In fact, they had prayed but not according to God's will. There are some prayers of Christians that God has not promised to answer (1 John 5:14).

The impropriety of their praying lay in the selfish intentions of their praying. What they were asking for was intended to be spent on their pleasures, which were hungering for gratification. Although they were more subtle than to pray outright for evil things, they may have asked for such things as money so as to spend it unworthily.

Some interpreters have sought for significance in the alternation between the middle and active voices in the three uses of the verb "ask" in verses 2 and 3: "...you do not ask [middle]...you ask [active]...you ask wrongly [middle]." The usual difference between these forms, however, is not readily seen in these statements. Mayor has argued that the active form implies using words without the spirit of prayer.[7] However, this leaves the reader with the curious thought that they were asking with the spirit of prayer (middle voice) but were doing so wrongly. A common use of the middle to imply "for yourselves" fits well with the third usage, "you are asking for yourselves wrongly,"[8] but it gives no satisfying explanation for the first use in the series: "You are not asking for yourselves," for that is precisely what they *were* doing. Stählin correctly asserts that it is virtually impossible to distinguish between the middle and the active of this verb in religious usage.[9] Consequently it is best here to see in the order—middle...active ...middle—a purely stylistic variation.

2. Friendship with the world (4:4–5)

a) This is hostility to God and is spiritual adultery (4:4)

7. Mayor, *James*, p. 138.

8. D. Edmond Hiebert, *The Epistle of James* (Chicago: Moody, 1979), p. 248 note.

9. Gustav Stählin, *"Aiteo,* TDNT, I, 192.

The oldest manuscript evidence has the word "adulteresses" alone.[10] Apparently the addition of "adulterers" (as in KJV, for example) was due to the undertstanding that the adultery was literal, and it was thought inappropriate to castigate only the female offenders. Assuming that the better-attested "adulteresses" is correct, one should view the passage as referring to spiritual adultery, whereby believers as the bride of Christ are guilty of unfaithfulness. The terminology is consistent with the words of Jesus (Matt. 12:39; 16:4; Mark 8:38). This use of figurative language has been preceded in the context by the metaphors of wars, battles, and killing.

"Friendship with the world" is the biblical definition of worldliness. It is the antithesis of love for God (cf. 1 John 2:15). In essence it is the demonstration of hostility toward God. Perhaps James was implying a contrast here to Abraham, whom he has earlier called "the friend of God" (2:23). If one's focus of attention is on the present world system, which is under Satan's sway (1 John 5:19), to that extent he has constituted himself in opposition to God. He has joined forces with the enemy. He is guilty of spiritual adultery. Thus James is viewing worldliness not just as the violation of a list of taboos but as an attitude of unfaithfulness to God. It is the condition of being lured away from complete loyalty to God in Christ by the attractions of the nonspiritual world system.

> b) *It violates the tenor of Scripture, which tells how God's Spirit is jealous for the total allegiance of the heart (4:5)*

Such disloyalty violates the clear teaching of the Scripture. Some interpreters have stated that the presence of the article with "Scripture" (*hē graphē*) demands that a specific quotation is

10. This is the reading of Aleph A B, as well as early representatives of the Old Latin, Syriac, and Coptic.

referred to.[11] Inasmuch as no Old Testament passage can be found to which the following words can be safely attributed as a quotation, one is driven either to predicating an unknown apocryphal work as the source, or some unknown version of the Old Testament. However, the usage of the definite article is not as restricted as has been suggested. Surely the uses of *hē graphē* in John 2:22 and 7:38 refer to a wider meaning of "Scripture" than one specific citation. James meant that the gist of Old Testament teaching supports this concept, just as persons may say today, "The Bible says," with the sense of "the Bible teaches," without intending to refer to a particular chapter and verse.

Although it has been suggested that verse 5 be separated into two sentences,[12] most interpreters continue to understand the last part of the verse as that which the Scripture teaches (to which the previous clause was referring).

The final clause of the verse is capable of being translated and interpreted in several ways. One possibility, supported by the Revised Standard Version, understands God as the subject who jealously yearns over the spirit (the human spirit), which He has made to dwell in us through creation. This takes the statement more generally and regards "in us" as "in us humans," rather than "in us Christians." A second possibility, reflected in the New American Standard Bible, sees God as yearning over the Holy Spirit, whom He has caused to dwell in all believers. It is difficult, however, to understand in what sense God would be yearning jealously over the Holy Spirit. A third understanding, found in the New English Bible rendering, regards the spirit as man's human spirit, implanted in man by creation, which turns toward envious desires. This statement, of course, is true, but it may not be the

---

11. J. B. Lightfoot, *The Epistle of St. Paul to the Galatians* (Grand Rapids: Zonderman, repr. 1965), pp. 147–148; P. H. Davids, *James*, p. 162.

12. Hiebert, *James*, p. 254. By this view, the first sentence is simply a question asking whether the readers foolishly suppose that Scripture speaks to no purpose when it teaches that one cannot love God and the world at the same time. The second sentence is then James's statement, and not a quotation.

best understanding of these words. The concept of God's causing *to pneuma* to dwell in us seems to refer more naturally to a special action regarding the Holy Spirit at regeneration, rather than to the general creation of the human spirit.

The best understanding is to regard the Holy Spirit as being meant in the words *to pneuma*, and to see these words as the subject of the sentence. Thus the rendering should be: "The Spirit which He has made to dwell in us jealously desires us" (NASB margin). The sense is that God wants our full allegiance, and the Holy Spirit—the representative of the Deity who indwells each Christian—performs that role of yearning for the believer's complete devotion. Anything less from us is spiritual adultery.

Those who object to this interpretation sometimes insist that the jealousy or envy (*pros phthonon*) mentioned here has negative connotations and is inappropriate of God. However, the metaphor of God as one jealous of all rivals is surely understandable, and the joining of this phrase with "desires" (*epipothei*) utilizes a term that appears exclusively in a good sense in its other New Testament occurrences.[13]

To summarize, James was explaining that Scripture was clear in its teaching that God's people are espoused to Him, and He is jealous for their complete devotion. The thought was contained in many Old Testament passages (Exod. 20:5; 34:14; Deut. 6:15; 32:19–21) and was repeated by Jesus (Matt. 22:37).

B. The Christian's Responsibility (4:6–17)

The problem facing believers is a formidable one indeed. The evil propensities that are present within each human find expression all too readily, even in the lives of Christians. Spiritual infidelity is a not-uncommon occurrence among those who have

13. Rom. 1:11; 2 Cor. 5:2, 9:14; Phil. 1:8, 2:26; 1 Thess. 3:6; 2 Tim. 1:4; 1 Peter 2:2.

claimed a committment to Christ. And this exists in spite of the fact that God has placed His Holy Spirit within His people to keep their allegiance and devotion to Him alive. What is to be done? What is the appropriate Christian response to the harsh realities of life in a less-than-perfect world and among not-yet-perfect saints?

1. Submit to God (4:6–10)

a) God continually provides more grace to make spiritual victory possible (4:6)

The responsibility for repudiating friendship with the world and giving wholehearted allegiance to Christ is not a hopeless one. The great encouragement for believers is that God does not cast us off when we stumble. Instead he gives more grace—more than enough to match the attractions of this world, more than sufficient to ward off the devil and overcome the flesh. By supplying His undeserved favor, which is the means of our victory, God expresses His yearning for His children and their spiritual welfare.

It was in the light of this truth that God has spoken in Scripture: "God is opposed to the proud, but gives grace to the humble." James has quoted the LXX rendering of Proverbs 3:34, a passage used also by Peter (1 Peter 5:5). It reminds the readers that those who proudly turn from God and choose to be friends of the world must face God's opposition. The world with its more immediate rewards ministers to their pride, and its wisdom can foster human egos and often advance their ambitions. God, however, ministers His grace to the humble. Those who are willing to acknowledge their need, repudiate selfish ambition, and let God's wisdom guide them will find that God's provision of grace for each day will be their greatest resource.

  b) *Believers should submit to God and resist the devil
     (4:7)*

In the light of the previous quotation, the readers are told to
abandon their pride and submit to God. "Submit" (*hupotagēte*)
involves more than "obey," although it obviously includes obedience. It indicates the surrender of the will to the leadership of
another. In this context it is the turning away from friendship
with the world and focusing upon the desires and will of God,
whose gracious love has won our hearts.

The corollary to this command to submission is the order to
resist the devil. "Resist" (*antistēte*) is essentially a defensive word,
meaning to withstand an attack. The Christian is not here instructed to go out and attack the devil by looking for new ways to
lure him into combat. It is assumed, rather, that the devil will do
the attacking. The Christian's responsibility is to walk with God,
carrying out His will in daily life according to the precepts of His
Word and warding off attacks and temptations from Satan when
they come.

At the same time there is a promise of victory: "... and he will
flee from you." Such a promise can be made because God has
provided the necessary spiritual armor and weapons (Eph. 6:10–17).
In conformity with the concept of "resisting" is the fact that the
armor described in Ephesians is all defensive, and the weapon (the
sword) can also be understood in this way. No doubt is expressed
by James as to the outcome of the encounter with Satan if the
believer truly submits to God and resists the devil. Careful
reflection upon personal experiences that have been less than
victorious will undoubtedly show a deficiency either in the depth
of one's commitment to God or one's faithfulness in employing
the means God has supplied for resisting the devil.

> *c) Sinners, especially sinning Christians, need to come in
>   faith and worship to God (4:8)*

"Draw near to God" is in contrasting parallel to the previous
statement, "Resist the devil," just as the next clause, "He will
draw near to you," is in contrast to the assertion regarding the
devil, "he will flee from you." To draw near to God was a common
Old Testament concept. It described the priests and their responsibilities (Exod. 19:22; Lev. 10:3; 21:21–23) in approaching the
tabernacle and its sacred ceremonies. The same word for "draw
near" (*engizō*) was also used in the LXX of all worshipers, and
that is surely the sense here (Isa. 29:13; Hos. 12:6). It was not an
evangelistic call but an appeal to believers who had been contami-
nated in some way by worldliness to return and give their full
allegiance to God. When they do, they will find that God is always
willing to meet them.

"Cleanse hands, O sinners" (literal) is a statement directed here
at sinning Christians. "Hands" is an appropriate metaphor for
outward activity, just as "hearts" in the next clause, "Purify
hearts, O double-minded ones," refers to inward thoughts and
attitudes. The victims of worldliness are sinners because they have
fallen short of God's standard, and they are double-minded because they are Christian and yet divided and inconsistent in their
thought and conduct.

> *d) Sin should be taken seriously and mourned over (4:9)*

Christians who sin are not to take it lightly. Three terms depict
the appropriate response. "Be miserable" (*talaipōrēsate*) is a verb
occurring only here in the New Testament, although the cognate
noun and adjective appear elsewhere. It describes the sense of
wretchedness and misery that sinning should produce in the lives
of those who have been redeemed. "Mourn" (*penthēsate*) specifies
the grieving and sorrow that a repentant sinner should experi-

150

Devout Jews in prayer at the Western Wall in Jerusalem.

ence. "Weep" (*klausate*) adds the element of outward display of sorrow. It is obvious that James is calling for genuine repentance, not some casual apology or mild expression of regret. The point is reinforced by additional command, "Let your laughter be turned into mourning, and your joy to gloom." There are times in life when laughter is inappropriate. The Old Testament speaks of "the laughter of the fool" (Eccles. 7:6) and indicates that loud cries of joy and mirth are not compatible with a state of penitence (Jer. 16:9). This does not contradict the New Testament teaching that rejoicing should be the Christian's continuing experience (1 Thess. 5:16). It is rather addressing the abnormal situation when worldliness has gained a foothold and must be repented of.

> e) *If believers humble themselves before the Lord, He will lift them up (4:10)*

This summarizing statement concludes the author's discussion of submission to God. He has shown that it involves resisting the efforts of the devil, drawing near to God in faith and worship, forsaking sinful deeds and thoughts, and acknowledging sinfulness with serious reflection and appropriate grief. All of this can be summed up by a command, "Humble yourselves[14] in the presence of the Lord." The readers are called upon to repent of worldly attitudes and sinful practices and to take their rightful position of submission and holiness before the Lord. Whether the reference to "the Lord" is to God (the Father) or to Christ may be debated. It is most likely, however, that James was not attempting to make a distinction here but was thinking of God as revealed in Christ. His point was that the ultimate answer to problems of worldly attitudes and the misdeeds that issue from them was not to give a list of prohibitions but to encourage complete devotion to God and His will, as revealed in Scripture and the gospel.

To this command was attached a promise, "and He will exalt you." This concept is not a new one to those familiar with the Scripture. The same thought occurs in the Old Testament (Job 5:11; Prov. 3:34; Isa. 40:3–4), and was stated three times by Jesus in words that James may have heard from His lips (Matt. 23:12; Luke 14:11; 18:14). The immediate attractions of the world must not be allowed to blind us to the prospect of God's far-greater compensation.

14. The aorist passive *tapeinōthēte* is frequently used with the sense of a middle. In this verb there is little difference in meaning between "humble yourselves" (middle) and "let yourselves be humbled" (passive).

Questions for Discussion

1. What are some wrong desires that cause conflicts among Christians?
2. How would you harmonize the apparent contradiction of "you do not ask" (4:2) with "you ask" (4:3), in regard to praying?
3. Who are the adulteresses of 4:4?
4. How does one go about submitting to God?
5. How does one "resist the devil"?
6. Does the devil always flee when Christians resist him?
7. How does James's emphasis on "mourning" over sin fit the Pauline teaching of continual Christian joy?

11

Planning Without God

James 4:11-17

Worldliness is far more subtle than some of its denouncers imply. James has identified loving the world as spiritual adultery. The clear biblical warning against loving the world is acknowledged by most Christians, but when the principle is applied to circumstances and activities, the consensus begins to crumble.

The disease of worldliness—the love for the world that is the antithesis of love for God—is recognized easily enough by some of its symptoms. Drunkenness, adultery, and lewdness are obvious examples. Many Christians add other items to their lists, such as certain forms of entertainment (but not all kinds); any form of drinking, smoking, dancing, certain kinds of recreation; certain kinds of dress, cosmetics, and Sunday activity. By no means are all lists the same, and few Christians have all these items on their list. Some will strongly oppose one set of actions, while others focus on another.

In James's treatment of this subject, which covers all of chapter 4, he has pointed out some different examples—ones not frequently thought of today as instances of worldliness, although they are very common. He has mentioned quarreling and strife as proceeding from thought patterns ("wisdom") that are worldly, not heavenly (4:1, cf. 3:14-17). He has called attention to envy and greed as other examples (4:2-3). Spiritual unfaithfulness, viewing sin lightly, and an arrogant manner are all instances of worldliness (4:4, 8–10).

In the next section (4:11–17), James continues to set forth instances, some of them seemingly innocent on the surface, that are nevertheless just as worldly and therefore harmful as the more popularly identified taboos. He talks about a critical spirit, which reflects itself in continually criticizing one's fellows. He writes about the making of plans that may appear to be reasonable and prudent but are actually worldly if God is ignored and unaided human wisdom is all that is employed. In the latter instance, it is not what is done that is wrong, but what is left undone. Worldliness is thus not only doing what is wrong, but not doing what is right. The doing or not doing are symptomatic of the heart condition, which acts or withholds actions on the basis of the kind of wisdom it is using.

2. Avoid judging others (4:11–12)

a) *Judging another person is actually a judging of the law (4:11)*

In the believer's attempts to resist worldly attitudes, he must submit to God not only in worship but also in obedience to His precepts, many of which deal with relations with other people. The practice of injurious speech that continually berates others is singled out for special mention.[1]

---

1. Verses 11 and 12 are related in thought to 2:1–13, and Oesterley notes how they follow more naturally after 2:12–13 than they do in their present position. "The General Epistle of James," EGT (Grand Rapids: Eerdmans, repr. ed.), IV, 461. However, there is no manuscript evidence to support the idea of a redaction or a misplacing of these verses, and their present position is not devoid of a contextual relationship.

The action here denounced is a continual speaking against other persons.[2] The verb carries the sense of speaking evil of, defaming, or slandering.[3] The emphasis seems to be more upon the idea of personal criticism and judgmental attitudes than with contradicting the content of an opponent's speech or position. It is an exhortation to avoid the spirit of censoriousness that Jesus also denounced (Matt. 7:1–5).

Are these words related to the context? Some see no connection at all, or at best only some appended thoughts.[4] They are viewed by such interpreters as of general application for all occasions. Davids sees the work of a redactor at this point.[5] One can hardly deny that the principle stated by James is true in all cases, and thus it is not inappropriate to apply these verses to a wide variety of instances. However, a connection with the context is not difficult to find. James has been discussing worldliness as evidenced by quarreling (4:1), envy (4:2), lack of humility (4:10), as well as selfish ambition (3:14–16) and the absence of peace (3:18). The believer's responsibility is to avoid contributing to this condition, and one of the key factors is the judicious use of speaking about one another.

To speak against a brother in this censorious way is to judge him. It is the same as saying that the speaker has already tried the case and is ready to announce the unfavorable verdict. But James adds the intriguing thought that such an act is to speak against

2. In the imperative, the present tense stresses continuing activity, which is then prohibited by the negative. Such a construction may mean either "continually avoid speaking against," or "do not continue speaking against" (i.e., "stop it").

3. Arndt, p. 413.

4. Bo Reicke, *The Epistle of James, Peter, and Jude,* in The Anchor Bible series (Garden City: Doubleday, 1964), p. 47; James Ropes, *The Epistle of St. James,* ICC (Edinburgh: T. & T. Clark, 1916), p. 273.

5. Peter H. Davids, *The Epistle of James,* NIGTC, Greek Testament Commentary series (Grand Rapids: Eerdmans, 1982), p. 169. However, if the words are as appropriate as Davids states, one wonders why he feels compelled to resort to a redactor. Why could not James himself have placed them where they are?

the law and to judge the law. The reference, of course, is to the Old Testament law that forbade talebearing and a nonloving spirit (Lev. 19:16, 18, and many other passages). James has previously cited the Old Testament injunction, "You shall love your neighbor as yourself" (2:8; cf. Lev. 19:18), and this passage may be uppermost in his mind here. When someone knows what God's Word commands and violates it anyway, he is saying in effect: "I have made a decision that this is not a good law, and therefore I will set it aside."

Such action, says James, means that one has taken himself out of the class of doers and has constituted himself a judge. The person with a critical spirit acts as if he can choose what parts of God's law he will obey and what aspects he may set aside. His performance gives the impression that he is not under God's law but over it.

Now, of course, this injunction does not relieve Christians of exercising discernment or forming opinions. What is clear is that the child of God must not become a talebearer nor bear false witness nor possess a critical spirit. Not all opinions need to be expressed!

b) Judging usurps the prerogatives of God, who is Lawgiver and Judge (4:12)

"One is Lawgiver and Judge" (literal), says James. The reference, of course, is to God. Ultimately it is God who has given man the true standards and who holds him accountable. It is He alone who not only made the law but has the authority to carry out all final judgment. These words are similar to the thought expressed by Jesus (Luke 12:4–5).

James's rhetorical question, "But who are you?," is based upon the indisputable truth of his previous assertion. Inasmuch as no reader would deny the ultimate authority of God to legislate and to judge, how can anyone suppose that he himself has the right to discredit his neighbor, impugn his motives, and denounce all who disagree with him? To do so is to display another form of worldliness—to act as if this world system were the only realm that exists, and that spiritual values and God's revelation can be ignored.

It must be understood, however, that James was not intending to prohibit believers from making any kind of moral judgments regarding each other. James himself has evaluated some instances of faulty conduct and called the perpetrators "sinners" (4:8). Even more severely does he castigate certain rich men (5:1–3). Scripture actually commands believers to evaluate the conduct of others and take appropriate action. Jesus told His followers not to treat spiritual truth carelessly by casting their "pearls before swine" (Matt. 7:6). Paul told the Corinthian Christians to judge sinfulness in their midst and excommunicate offenders (1 Cor. 5:1–5). They were to reject association with so-called brothers who persisted in immoral living (1 Cor. 5:11). John instructed his readers to put visiting teachers to the test and make the appropriate decisions about them (1 John 4:1). Teachers of falsehood were to be refused any kind of welcome or support (2 John 10–11). What James was therefore prohibiting was a judgmental spirit that usurped authority belonging to God.

3. Stop planning without God (4:13–17)

James gives yet another exhortation to help believers avoid that worldliness that is hostile to God. In spite of the conclusion of some, such as Oesterley, that "vv. 13–17 form an independent section entirely unconnected with what precedes or follows,"[6] the thought of the section fits clearly into the proposition of James that a love of the world is hostile to God because it ignores His will.

---

6. Oesterley, *James*, p. 462.

> *a) Elaborate planning of mundane matters without regard*
> *for God fails to consider the fleeting nature of human*
> *life (4:13–14)*

VERSE 13. The paragraph is introduced by the interjection "Come!" or "Come now" (*age nun*), used in the New Testament only here and in 5:1.[7] The following illustration depicts industrious businessmen who make careful and elaborate plans without any regard for God. The various activities may not be improper, but if God is ignored, they are worldly.

These energetic Jewish traders have precisely scheduled their travel plans ("today or tomorrow"), the exact location of their enterprise ("such and such a city"—can you not visualize a finger pointing it out on the map?), the duration of this intended operation ("spend a year there"), the precise nature of their activity ("engage in business" [KJV, "buy and sell"]), and the anticipated outcome ("make a profit").

This picture of traveling Jewish businessmen was not unusual in the first century. Travel, while not comfortable or luxurious by modern standards, was nevertheless regularly done. The New Testament itself reveals the readiness with which Paul could travel great distances. An example from the business world is the situation of Aquila and Priscilla, whose travels can be reconstructed from the New Testament data:

Pontus to Rome
Rome to Corinth (Acts 18:2–3)
Corinth to Ephesus (Acts 18:18–19)
Ephesus to Rome (Rom. 16:3–5)
Rome to Ephesus (2 Tim. 4:19)

---

7. The term *age* is actually a present imperative second person singular but is used regularly in this form, even with plurals, as here. The word is listed as a separate entry in Arndt and designated as an interjection.

A soft-drink merchant in Jerusalem.

It must not be concluded that James was condemning wise planning. Jesus taught His followers the folly of failing to calculate one's resources before beginning some enterprise (Luke 14:28–32). What is denounced is planning that leaves God out, planning that thinks human ingenuity alone is all that is necessary.

VERSE 14. Here James reminds his readers that their knowledge of what will happen "tomorrow" is not certain enough to allow them the luxury of making such firm plans. No man, aside from one with a special prophetic gift, can predict the future with absolute certainty. Even life itself is precarious.

161

Various schemes of punctuation have been proposed for this verse.[8] One of the most common regards "tomorrow" as the end of a sentence, with "what" being an interrogative introducing a separate question. Hence the New International Version renders it this way: Why, you do not even know what will happen tomorrow. What is your life?" The King James is similar. The New American Standard Bible, renders all of the above as one sentence: "Yet you do not know what your life will be like tomorrow." This latter way of rendering the text is objected to by Ropes because it seems to raise the question of the *conditions* of their life on the morrow, whereas the remainder of the verse shows that the uncertainty of *life itself* was what James had in mind.[9] It is true that *poia* is not the simple interrogative "what?" but "of what kind?" or "what sort of?" Hence James was not asking a philosophical question, "What is your life?" (κjv), but a more descriptive one, "What sort of life do you have?" It does seem, however, that the answer to such a question could well be: "Your life is transitory, precarious, and not totally controllable or predictable." This is precisely the answer James gives, and it was not inappropriate, regardless of which punctuation one chooses.

The latter punctuation is preferred by this writer, and it is the choice of the UBS Greek text. The phrase "that which pertains to tomorrow" (*to tēs aurion*) is regarded as an accusative of reference, and the words "of what sort your life will be" constitute a noun clause serving as the direct object of the verb "know." An appropriate translation would be: ". . . [you] who know not regarding tomorrow what sort of life you will have."

The reason why man's knowledge of the future and his planning for extended projects are permeated with uncertainties is that his very life is transitory at best. The same thought was expressed in

8. The UBS text lists four possibilities that have been discovered among various manuscripts or proposed by editors.

9. J. Ropes, *James*, p. 278.

Proverbs 27:1. James reminds these spiritually insensitive businessmen, "You are a vapor" (NIV, "mist"). Like the steam that
escapes from a pan cooking over the fire, or the breath that is
briefly visible on a cold morning, so life itself has its time of
visibility; but in the light of God's eternal plan, the earthly
manifestation is brief. The man who makes his earthly plans
without sensitivity to the nature of life itself is clearly foolish and
spiritually ignorant.

b) Proper planning submits all plans to God's will (4:15)

The thought of verse 13 is resumed. James was writing to
people who held to the statement in verse 13 instead of the one in
verse 15.

The error of these readers was not in what they said but in what
was left unsaid. They should have taken God into their planning
and have submitted everything to Him. "If the Lord wills" would
have been an acknowledgment that the planners wanted God's
direction and approval and would do nothing without them.

Numerous instances exist in the New Testament where such
statements were expressed in conjunction with human plans. Paul
told the Jews at Ephesus that he would return for a renewed
ministry among them "if God wills" (Acts 18:21). He wrote to the
Corinthians that he planned another visit to them "if the Lord
wills" (1 Cor. 4:19), and that he would remain with them a
considerable time "if the Lord permits" (1 Cor. 16:7). A similar
thought is doubtless to be inferred from Paul's statement that he
hoped "in the Lord" to send Timothy to Philippi" (Phil. 2:19) and
trusted "in the Lord" to go to Philippi himself in the near future
(Phil. 2:24). The writer of Hebrews expressed the goal of reaching
spiritual maturity with the readers "if God permits" (Heb. 6:3).

It would be wrong, however, to imagine that James was insisting
upon a ritualistic formula to be attached to every statement that

involved some future action. There are other instances in the New Testament where plans are stated without these words. In Ephesus, Paul stated his intention of visiting Rome after traveling to Jerusalem, Macedonia, and Achaia, he did not append this formula (Acts 19:21). He told the Romans about his plan to visit Rome on his way to Spain and likewise did not attach this proviso (Rom. 15:24–28). What James was talking about, and what Paul demonstrated by his own practice, was the need for a proper attitude. When one's perspective is correct, it will be reflected at times in words but always shows in the way he looks at life and makes his plans.

The text also indicates that the believer must recognize his dependence upon God's will for two factors—not just the accomplishment of the planned activity but also for life itself. Not only are we unable to plan business ventures (or any other kind) with complete certainty, but we cannot be sure that we will even be alive to start the project, much less finish it. The child of God needs to view life from the right perspective, not only in salvation matters but regarding every aspect of his existence.

In addition it should be noted the James finds nothing wrong with planning. One element in the prescribed conduct is to be able to say, "We will do this or that." Absence of a plan is no virtue. What is faulty is the sort of planning that fails to touch all the bases. Leaving God outside the picture is the grievous error.

> *c) Glorying in worldly pursuits is evil, even if no misdeeds are committed (4:16–17)*

VERSE 16. These worldly businessmen were boasting about their abilities and plans, instead of following the biblically authorized manner (Jer. 9:23–24). The term "boast" (*kauchasthe*) denotes self-glorying, almost always in a bad sense.[10] The only legitimate

10. See the excellent discussion of this term by R. Bultmann in TDNT, III, 645–654.

boasting by the Christian should be after the example of Paul, who boasted "in Christ Jesus" as the One who had made possible all of his apostolic accomplishments (Rom. 15:17; 2 Cor. 10:8, 13, 17). Self-glorying keeps the credit to oneself and fails to give the glory to God, who is the source of all wisdom, strength, and ability.

More specifically they were glorying in their "arrogance." The term *alazoneiais* is a plural and refers to repeated displays of arrogance by these self-confident merchants. The word family describes the activity of one who makes more of himself than the facts warrant. By his words or his attitude he arouses expectations that are unrealistic.[11] The noun appears only here and in 1 John 2:16. The latter instance describes the man whose worldly attitude makes him ignore God and suppose that he is in control of earthly affairs—not realizing that the world is passing away. The adjective form also occurs twice, both times in lists in which the term is associated with a word also denoting pride or haughtiness (*hyperephanos*; Rom. 1:30; 2 Tim. 3:2). The basic idea of James's term is pretentiousness or arrogance. These merchants were proud of their abilities, made no secret of the fact, and conveyed the impression that they were fully capable of accomplishing by their own abilities whatever they set out to do.

All such boasting, says James, is evil. It is not only socially irritating and demonstrably foolish but contrary to God's revealed truth and disobedient to His commands. It is the display of human vanity by those who have thought only of themselves with no thought for God. It is evil because it does not glorify God.

VERSE 17. The discussion is summed up in a statement that could have been a well-known proverb. At least, it is a pithy saying that lends itself well to such a use. A literal rendering would be "Therefore, to one knowing to do a good thing and not doing [it], to him it is sin." Worldliness is an attraction to the world that causes God to be omitted from one's plan. What is sobering about

11. G. Delling, "Alazon, alazoneia," TDNT, I, 226–227.

it is the fact that it is not just an unfortunate omission; it is sin. Sins of omission are sinful nonetheless, just as if they were actual misdeeds. The same principle was stated in the Old Testament by Samuel, who called failure to pray a "sin against the LORD" (1 Sam. 12:23).

Questions for Discussion

1. How would you define worldliness in the light of biblical principles?
2. Under what circumstances is it right to judge another person?
3. Why is someone with a critical spirit actually judging God's law?
4. Should the Christian ever make plans, or merely wait for God to bring all circumstances to pass?
5. Can a person sin if he does not actually do something wrong?

12

When Money Is Misused

James 5:1–12

Tensions between the wealthy and the poor have been occurring for a long time. Twentieth-century outcries are no new phenomena. In Bible times there was usually not a middle class in society, and the gulf between the rich and the poor could be very wide.

The Bible does not denounce money *per se*, or rich men as such. It does not call all money "filthy lucre," only that which is acquired by shameful means (the epithet literally means "shameful gain"). Scripture does not designate money as the "root of all evil"; it is the "love of money" that received this opprobrium (1 Tim. 6:10). Rich men who receive God's disapproval are defined not simply as people with much money, but as those "who trust in riches" (Prov. 11:28; Mark 10:24, KJV). Many wealthy persons are clearly described in the Bible with divine approval, and in some cases it is stated that their wealth was a blessing God had given them (Gen. 12:2; 13:2; 24:35; Job 1:1–3, 10; 42:10–13).

Those who carefully read the Bible understand that wealth is a stewardship entrusted to men to use wisely. The God who has made us and has supplied us resources with which to function also holds us accountable for how we carry out our stewardship (1 Tim. 6:17–19). Have we used these resources for His glory? For the furtherance of His program? For the benefit of others and not just ourselves?

Wealth itself is a relative term. All of us know persons who are economically better off than we, and we tend to regard them as "rich" in contrast to ourselves. At the same time, others less affluent than ourselves may think of us as the "rich" ones. Experience in traveling abroad quickly brings the recognition that Americans are more affluent than much of the world and makes one wonder about the exercise of his own stewardship.

Problems regarding rich and poor loomed large in James's thinking. He has referred to them in 1:9–11, 2:1–13, to some extent in 4:13–17, and now more severely in 5:1–6. The principles he sets forth merit every Christian's careful attention.

VII. Warning to Currupt Rich Men (5:1–6)

A. The Judgment of These Rich Men (5:1–3)

1. Their coming judgment should cause them to wail now (5:1)

"Come now" (*age nun*) is the second of the two New Testament uses of this interjection (see 4:13). It summons the ones addressed to give careful attention to what will be said.

Who were these rich persons being addressed? The wealthy men mentioned in 1:10–11 were most likely members of the Christian assembly. However, the rich visitor of 2:2 was probably not. If these persons in 5:1 were viewed as part of the Christian group, it seems clear that they must have been merely professed believers, for the fires of judgment are described as destroying both them and their riches. It is better to understand these rich men as oppressive landowners who were not believers. They are not challenged to repent but merely to wail over their certain prospect. They are viewed with a prophetic eye as already receiving the fires of judgment.

168

The strongest objection to regarding them as non-Christians is the fact that they are directly addressed in a letter to Christians. Would such persons ever see this Epistle? Had James forgotten who his audience was? Such a circumstance, however, is not as unusual as it may seem. The Epistle of James is steeped in Old Testament terminology and style, and remarks directed to Israel's oppressors were a common feature of the Prophets. Isaiah delivered a message to Babylon and that nation was told to wail (13:6). He also gave prophecies to Philistia (14:28ff.), to Moab (15:1ff.), to Damascus (17:1ff.), to Ethiopia (18:1ff.), and to Tyre and Sidon (23:1ff.). Ezekiel addressed messages to Ammon (25:1ff.), Tyre (26:1—28:19), Sidon (28:20–24), and Egypt (chaps. 29–32). It is highly unlikely that those nations ever heard or read those prophecies. Their primary purpose, however, was to provide encouragement for Israel by letting that nation know that God would ultimately deal with her oppressors. In similar fashion, James's Christian readers were being informed that God would judge oppression at the proper time, and believers must not become disillusioned nor look enviously at the rich who might attend their services.

Eastern people are very demonstrative in grief. James challenged them to weep (*klausate*) by howling (*ololyzontes*) over the miseries (*talaipōriais*) coming upon them. Neither here nor in the words to follow is there any call to repentance. To the contrary, James thunders out like an Old Testament prophet and regards the fires of judgment as already in process against these persons.

2. Their ill-gotten wealth is already corrupted (5:2–3a)

Verse 2. Wealth in biblical times was commonly held in grain and other foodstuffs, in clothing, and in precious metals, as well as in flocks and herds. It may be that the first three are referred to here. "Your riches have rotted" may refer to hoarded grain stored in great barns (Luke 12:15–21). Although far more than the owner could use, he failed to share his largess with others. The "moth-eaten" garments were likewise worthless, even though in life they were viewed as indications of great wealth. Of course, as these wealthy men looked at their goods, it did not appear to them this way at all. Their barns were well cared for and the grain protected. Their robes sparkled with lavish care and the finest of fabrics. James was looking with a prophet's eye, seeing things from God's point of view. He saw judgment as already in progress and man's opulence revealed as temporal at best, subject to swift destruction.

VERSE 3a. Even the gold and silver are seen as having rusted. In the physical world, rust does not affect gold or silver, and though silver may tarnish, gold does not even do that. In actuality the rich owners would have kept their valuables polished and sparkling. Again, however, we must allow James the privilege of bold metaphor as he describes the scene of final judgment in striking figures that arrest the attention and drive home the point. The meaning is clear: what men think is so important may be spiritually worthless.

3. Their wealth will testify against them (5:3b)

In the judgment, their corrupted wealth will stand as a witness to their misuse of God's provision. No excuses will undo the evidence of their hoarded wealth, which was used only for selfish luxury, not for assisting others. In the bold and even bizarre imagery that apocalyptic prophets were noted for, James describes the rust of their corroded gold and silver as destined to eat their flesh as fire.[1] The fires of judgment will be fueled by this

---

1. "Your flesh" (*tas sarkas humōn*) is plural, and is explained by some as a reference to the fleshy parts of the body. So J. B. Mayor, *The Epistle of St. James* (Grand Rapids: Zondervan, repr. 1913 ed.), p. 156. Arndt, however, explains the plural as denoting flesh in the mass, while the singular denotes the substance (p. 750). There is no compelling reason why the plural for flesh here cannot mean the same thing as "bodies."

corrupted wealth, instances of which are described in the succeeding verses.

The folly of their action is stated in the clause, "You have stored up treasure[2] in the last days." Note that James said, "*in* the last days (Greek)," not "*for* the last days" (KJV). He understood, in agreement with other New Testament writers, that the "last days" was a designation for messianic times, which began with Christ's first coming (Acts 2:16–17; 1 Tim. 4:1; 2 Peter 3:3; 1 John 2:18). These rich men were oblivious to the momentous days in which they were living. They did not understand that the "last days" had already begun and that Christ's second coming could be at any moment. They were like the Babylonians, feasting and reveling in willful ignorance that disaster was about to strike their city (Dan. 5:1–31).

B. The Corrupt Deeds of These Rich Men (5:4–6)

1. They withheld the wages of their farm workers (5:4)

James has been castigating the rich for their hoarded wealth. Now he shows where that wealth had come from. In some cases wealthy landowners had withheld the wages that had been honestly earned by their field workers. Manuscript evidence varies between two similarly spelled words—one meaning "withheld" and the other "stolen, robbed, or defrauded."[3] If the more widely attested

---

2. J. Ropes objects to this translation because it leaves the verb *ethēsaurisate* (you stored up, you treasured) without an object. *Epistle of St. James* (Edinburgh: T. & T. Clark, 1916), p. 287. However, this fails to take into account its uses in Luke 12:21 and 2 Cor. 12:14, where it is clear that no further object is necessary.

3. *aphusterēmenos* (withheld) is found in Aleph and B, and adopted by the UBS 2nd edition and Nestle; *apesterēmenos* (stolen, robbed, defrauded) is found in A B[2] P, most minuscules, and is adopted by the UBS 3rd edition.

Farm worker winnowing grain near Bethlehem.

reading is adopted,[4] the sense is that the landowners had cheated their workers by refusing to pay all that was owed.

Such shameful conduct was sufficiently common in biblical times that the Mosaic law contained regulations prohibiting it, and numerous prophetic voices were raised against it (Lev. 19:13; Deut. 24:14–15; Job 7:1–2; 24:10; 31:38–40; Jer. 22:13; Mal. 3:5). One of Jesus' parables reflected the proper practice of paying workers daily (Matt. 20:1–16).

The wages of these defrauded workers cry out—not from the pockets of those to whom they rightfully belonged but from the coffers of the wealthy owner who was profiting at their expense.

4. Bruce M. Metzger explains that a majority of the UBS 3rd edition editors preferred the more widely attested reading *apesterēmenos* (defrauded), and regarded *aphusterēmenos* (withheld), which appears only in Aleph and B (representatives of a single type of text), as an Alexandrian refinement. Their choice was given a C rating. *A Textual Commentary on the Greek New Testament* (London: UBS, 1971), pp. 684–685.

Coupled with the witness of these diverted funds were the outcries of the workers themselves. Those who "reaped" (NASB, "did the harvesting") are apparently the same as those who "mowed," mentioned earlier in the sentence. These cries for justice have not gone unnoticed by God. He is here designated by one of His frequent Old Testament titles, "Lord of hosts" (NASB, marg.) or "Lord of armies." As Burdick has reminded us, "In 1 Samuel 17:45 it refers to the armies of Israel. The word 'host' is also used to refer to God's angels (2 Chron. 18:18) and to all the stars (Deut. 4:19). God is Lord of the armies of earth, of the angelic armies, and of all the starry host. This is a graphic way of declaring that God is almighty."[5] When this almighty God hears the outcries of the oppressed, something will surely be done.

2. They lived in luxury and wanton indulgence (5:5)

A second example of their misuse of money is the selfishness and unwarranted opulence with which the wealthy indulged themselves. The first verb (*etruphēsate*) occurs only here in the New Testament and means "to lead a life of luxury of self-indulgence." There are times in the Old Testament (LXX) when it is used in a good sense (Ps. 37:4, 11; Isa. 55:2). In this context of James, it has the negative connotation of using wealth solely for display or personal whim. The second verb (*espatalēsate*) always has a bad connotation. It describes a life of wanton, wasteful indulgence. Paul used it of the pleasure-seeking widow who "is dead even while she lives" (1 Tim. 5:6). In stark contrast to the defrauded harvesters, these opulent owners were living lavishly.

With biting irony James says to them, "You have fattened your hearts in a day of slaughter." Like ignorant cattle who are encouraged to eat well just before being led to the slaughter-

5. Donald W. Burdick, "James," EBC (Grand Rapids: Zondervan, 1981), XII, 200.

house, these men seem blissfully ignorant of impending judgment. The thought is similar to that expressed in 5:3b.

The "day of slaughter" has an eschatological sense in this passage, in the light of the contextual references to the "last days" (v. 3), "the coming of the Lord" (vv. 7–8), and the "Judge...standing right at the door" (v. 9). The Old Testament background for the expression is found in such passages as Isaiah 34:2, Jeremiah 12:3, and Ezekiel 21:15.

3. They condemned and killed the righteous (5:6)

A third instance of the misuse of wealth and the power it provided was the persecution directed against the righteous. The same theme was mentioned in 2:6, where the rich were the ones who oppressed and dragged the righteous poor to court.

Because the term "righteous" is a singular,[6] it may be wondered whether the reference is to Christ, who is called "the Righteous One" in Acts 3:14 (also Acts 7:52; 22:14; 1 John 2:1). This seems unlikely, however, for this Epistle was written to the Diaspora, not to Jerusalem Jews who may have participated in the scheme to crucify Jesus. Furthermore, the practice of the rich in exploiting the poor, even sometimes to the point of death, was often denounced by the prophets and would have been familiar to Jewish readers everywhere (Amos 2:6, 5:10–12; Ps. 10:8–9; Isa. 3:14–15; 57:1). The episode of Ahab, Jezebel, and Naboth provided a graphic example (1 Kings 21:1–16). The singular expression, "the righteous man," is best explained as the generic use of the article to denote the whole class of similar persons.

The closing sentence, "He does not resist you," is a dramatic, forceful close to this sobering discussion. Some wish to treat it as a question, with an affirmative answer expected, "Does he not

6. *ton dikaion*

resist you?"[7] The resistance is usually viewed as the witness of the righteous against the wicked in the day of judgment.

It is more convincing to this commentator, however, to regard the words as a declaration that the righteous victim does not resist the oppressor, and this makes the violent attack against him all the more outrageous.[8] He does not resist, either because he is defenseless, or because he has adopted the principles of his Master (Matt. 5:39–42). Either way, the viciousness of the oppressor stands out in starkest contrast to the righteous character of the victim.

To possess money brings with it serious responsibility. The potential for misuse is great. James has made it clear that God holds men accountable for how they use it.

VIII. Miscellaneous Exhortations (5:7–20)

A. Facing Hostility (5:7–12)

In this concluding section of James, several matters are raised that deal with issues Christians frequently face. The first of these arose naturally out of the previous discussion. Believers must learn how to respond to hostility, whether from wealthy oppressors (5:1–6) or from anyone else.

1. The Exhortation (5:7a)

7. J. Ropes, *James,* p. 292; Peter H. Davids, *The Epistle of St. James,* NIGTC (Grand Rapids: Eerdmans, 1981), p. 180.

8. J. B. Mayor, *James,* pp. 160–161; James B. Adamson, *The Epistle of St. James,* NICNT (Grand Rapids: Eerdmans, 1976), pp. 188–189.

Farm workers washing and packing potatoes at Tirzah.

Among the words for "patience" that occur in the New Testament, the one in this command, "Be patient, therefore, brethren," stresses non-retaliation. It means to hold one's spirit in check. "Restrain your temper" is the idea. The believer is not to allow mistreatment and oppression to drive him to hatred, bitterness, or despair. Such feelings might be directed against the persons causing the pressure, or against God, who was allowing it to happen.

This non-retaliatory acceptance must be the response "until the coming of the Lord." James was referring to the return of Christ, which he thought might occur at any time. That understanding of Christ's promise was correct and should be the attitude of every Christian. His attitude was not mistaken. Although James set no dates, he recognized that Jesus had commanded His followers to maintain a spirit of watchfulness, and he was conveying that to his readers. Until Jesus comes and rights all wrongs, the Christian's obligation is to leave vengeance with Him and meanwhile maintain a patient spirit.

2. Three Illustrations (5:7b–11)

a) The example of the farmer (5:7b–9)

VERSE 7b. The illustration of the farmer is drawn from Palestinian agriculture, with which James and most of his first readers were very familiar. He described the farmer as sowing seed on ground that experienced no rain at all during much of the year. The fields were brown and the soil was dry. Modern irrigation techniques were unknown, and dependence upon the rains was the only resource. Therefore, he must accept that factor and plan accordingly.

The phrase "early and late rains"[9] refers to the fall rains in October and November, which soften the ground after the blistering heat of summer, and to the spring showers of April and May, which enable the grain to ripen.[10] This reference to well-known features of Palestinian climate (Deut. 11:14; Jer. 5:24; Joel 2:23) takes no notice of the heavy winter rains, which also fall on that land. The subject of the verb "gets," or "receives," is probably "it," referring to "the earth" (*tēs gēs*), rather than to the fruit (which does not exist when the early rains fall). The subject could also be "he," referring to the farmer.

VERSE 8. In like manner, the believer who is facing hostility must demonstrate a willingness to wait for vindication, rather than retaliate in some fashion. As wise and knowledgeable farmers

9. A textual variant occurs here in the Greek text. The best attested reading, supported by both Alexandrian and Western text types, omits "rains." Alternative readings supply either "rain" or "fruit." "Rains" is certainly the word to be supplied by the readers' understanding, in the light of the well-known OT expression.

10. J. Ropes, *James*, pp. 295–296.

who must await the life-giving rains for the crops, Christians must live in anticipation of their Lord's coming and not become upset at circumstances during the waiting.

The coming of the Lord was a very real prospect to James. It was "at hand" (literally, "has come near"). Even though he died without experiencing Christ's coming, he was correct in understanding that with Christ's first coming, God's prophetic calendar has begun. Messianic times had started. James did not know the exact date of the second coming, and neither do we. But our anticipation should be as strong as his.

VERSE 9. Hostility from others is not easily endured. James was well aware of the human propensity to lash out in retaliation, or at least to complain against real or imagined instigators. "Do not groan" (*literally; mē stenazete*) utilizes a verb meaning to sigh or groan, with a feeling internal and largely unexpressed because of a condition one is suffering from and longs to be free of (Rom. 8:23–26). There may be audible sounds, but actual words are not usually involved. As James uses it here, therefore, the reference "is to inner sighing not to open complaints,"[11] even though the focus is against others (*kat' allēlōn*).

James warns the readers that to groan with complaints against others is the sort of judging spirit he has been cautioning them about (4:11–12). "That you yourselves may not be judged" seems clearly indebted to the words of Jesus, which James may have heard (Matt. 7:1–5). Even inward feelings of bitterness and criticism that may not be outwardly expressed are capable of accurate judgment by the One to whom we are responsible.

The reminder that "the Judge is standing right at the door" should be a caution that judgment may not be some hazy, theoretical, far-distant event. In the momentous era of the last days—a time that James understood as now present in some sense—proper conduct and the Christian's accountability are highly significant matters.

11. J. Schneider, "Stenazo," TDNT, VII, 603.

b) The example of the prophets (5:10)

The second illustration of the proper way to face hostility takes the readers to the Old Testament prophets. Most of them were persecuted severely in their lifetime, despite the fact that they were God's messengers. Jesus once gave His listeners the same illustration: "Blessed are you when men cast insults at you, and persecute you, and say all kinds of evil against you falsely, on account of Me. Rejoice, and be glad, for your reward in heaven is great, for so they persecuted the prophets who were before you" (Matt. 5:11–12). Stephen likewise took his hearers to the prophets for an example: "Which one of the prophets did your fathers not persecute? And they killed those who had previously announced the coming of the Righteous One . . ." (Acts 7:52).

One of the best-known Old Testament prophets who suffered hostility during his ministry was Jeremiah. That godly prophet was beaten and put in the stocks (Jer. 20:2), placed into prison (32:2), and thrown into a muddy cistern (38:6). Such prophets accepted their evil treatment and did not abandon their faith in God or the performance of their ministry. They proclaimed the Lord's message under His authority and direction, even though it did not exempt them from suffering.

c) The example of Job (5:11)

The thought now moves slightly from patience as a non-retaliatory spirit (*makrothumia*) to patience as steadfast endurance (*hupomonē*). James seems to be remembering the Beatitude given by Jesus in the Sermon on the Mount (Matt. 5:12) as he writes, "We count those blessed who endured."

The endurance (*tēn hupomonēn*) of Job as one whose stand for God was shaken by circumstances around him was acknowledged by Jews everywhere. His righteousness had been remarked upon by Ezekiel (14:4). It is not without significance that James did not use *makrothumia* (longsuffering, patience) here, for Job was not always free from complaint.[12] "Let the day perish on which I was to be born" (3:3), and "Why did I not die at birth?" (3:11) were two of his many cries of anguish. He showed himself to be very human in his feelings of frustrations. The important point to note, however, is that his basic faith in God did not waver. He never succumbed to his wife's suggestion to "curse God and die" (2:9). He endured incredible suffering, insensitivity from his counselors, and misunderstanding at home, but he continued to trust God through it all.

The readers had also seen "the outcome of the Lord's dealings." "Outcome" (*telos*) can mean either "goal, purpose" or "end, result, outcome." Inasmuch as the next clause appears to be explanatory ("that....") and names the outcome of the whole experience, it is best to regard *telos* as meaning "result." The outcome for Job meant great blessing for him and was also a refutation of Satan's accusation. The anguished sufferer learned that "the Lord is full of compassion and is merciful." Even though circumstances seemed exactly opposite to this, Job's endurance enabled him to see that God's blessings were abundant if one was willing to let God choose the time to bestow them. Eventually God doubled Job's possessions and doubled the number of his children, for the original ten were not permanently lost to him and would be restored at the resurrection (Job 42:10–17).

3. A final caution (5:12)

In spite of the fact that Oesterley sees "not the remotest connection between this verse and the section that has gone just

---

12. This fact leads Davids to conclude that James was not thinking of the canonical record of Job, but of other popular traditions regarding him, such as found in the apocryphal *Testament of Job*, which completely omits the complaints of Job. However, the explanation given above seems reasonable and avoids putting James in conflict with another part of canonical Scripture. Davids, *James*, p. 187; *The Testament of Job*, ed. Robert A. Kraft (Missoula, MT: Scholars Press, 1974).

before,"[13] and Davids thinks "a specific connection to anything which precedes is unlikely,"[14] the use of the conjunction *de* (but, and, moreover) suggests some sort of continuity. Surely the practice of indiscriminate oathtaking to reinforce one's defense during some hostile confrontation was a legitimate subject for James to mention at this point.

The literal "before all things" (*pro pantōn*) hardly means that this particular matter is worse than murder or adultery. Rather it must be connected to the context. The meaning is that in all one's attempts to avoid expressing impatience toward tormentors, he should first of all avoid swearing. It may be admitted that "cursing" (calling down imprecations from God upon someone) might be more readily understood here, but the term used meant "to take an oath" (*omnuete*). In times of oppression or persecution, one may be tempted to deny his guilt by reinforcing his statement with an oath. This is precisely what Peter did when he was accused by a servant girl of being a follower of Jesus (Matt. 26:72). An oath calls upon God as a witness to one's statement and implicates Him to punish the swearer if falsehood is spoken.

The believer is commanded to refrain from swearing "by heaven or by earth or with any other oath." The word of the Christian should be so trustworthy that his "yes" will always mean "yes" and his "no" will mean "no." This command by James repeats the teaching of Jesus, although not in exactly the same words recorded by Matthew (5:33–37). Our Lord gave the explanation that varying the authority by which one swore (so as to avoid the name of God and perhaps leave a loophole for non-compliance) implicated God just the same. Furthermore, to swear by one's own head implied that failure to comply with the oath would bring some catastrophe upon him, but this is not within man's control.

Much evidence exists that oathtaking was greatly abused at that time—not only in the form of profanity, whereby God's name was

13. W. E. Oesterley, "The General Epistle of James," EGT, IV, 472.
14. P. Davids, *James*, p. 188.

employed meaninglessly in flippant swearing, but also in the clever schemes of the rabbis to explain some formulas as more binding than others. It had become so rampant that the Essenes prohibited all taking of oaths. Josephus said: "Every word they speak is more binding than an oath; they avoid swearing as something worse than perjury among other people, for they say a man is already condemned if he cannot be believed even without swearing by God."[15] A section of the Mishnah is devoted to the subject of various kinds of oaths and the degree to which each was binding.[16]

Should the taking of an oath in the courtroom be exempted from this prohibition? Most exegetes think so, not because they find compelling reasons in the statements of James or Jesus, but because of Old Testament practice in which some oaths were commanded, and because of the examples of oathtaking by God, Jesus, and perhaps Paul. It must be acknowledged that the main focus of James's words did not seem to have the courtroom in mind so much as the everyday relations of Christians in a hostile world.

It is nevertheless difficult to see how any oaths can be eliminated from the scope of this command. James said, "Do not swear...with any...oath." Jesus said, "Make no oath at all" (Matt. 5:34). That this was an absolute prohibition was understood by Clement of Alexandria at the beginning of the third century, when he wrote regarding the true Gnostic (that is, the true Christian):

15. Josephus, *The Jewish War,* 2.8.6 (134). However, Josephus also gives the information several paragraphs later that the Essenes "swear great oaths" at their initiation into the group (*Jewish War,* 2.8.7 [139]).

16. *The Mishnah,* trans. Herbert Danby, (London: Oxford Univ. 1933), Fourth Division: "Shebuoth" ("Oaths"), pp. 408–421. The Mishnah is the body of Jewish law transmitted orally. It was compiled in the late second century by Rabbi Judah the Prince.

But he does not even swear, preferring to make averment, in affirmation by "yea," and in denial by "nay" .... It suffices, then, with him, to add to an affirmation or denial the expression "I say truly," for confirmation to those who do not perceive the certainty of his answer. For he ought, I think, to maintain a life calculated to inspire confidence towards those without, so that an oath may not even be asked.[17]

Other church fathers on record as disapproving all oathtaking are Tertullian, Origen, Gregory of Nazianzus, and Chrysostom.[18] The contemporary Mennonite author D. Edmond Hiebert writes: "Committed to the principle that his speech should be totally honest under all circumstances, the believer can maintain that court oaths become unnecessary."[19]

Some of those who see here a prohibition of all oaths regard the New Testament as having superseded the old in some sense, as true light supersedes shadow.[20] The unique position of the divine Jesus Christ makes the problems inherent in human oathtaking inapplicable to him. As for Paul's use of the oath, it may be questioned whether there is an instance of a true oath in any of Paul's statements.

Regardless of how far one applies the prohibition, the point is clear that the believer's word should always be trustworthy without the need of an oath to make it believable. If reaction against accusers causes one to implicate God in his defense and to demand that God prove His support by some direct intervention

17. Clement of Alexandria, *The Stromata,* 7.8 in *The Ante-Nicene Fathers,* ed. Alexander Roberts and James Donaldson (Grand Rapids: Eerdmans, repr. 1979), II, 537.

18. Fred. W. Benedict, "Oaths," *The Brethren Encyclopedia* (Philadelphia: 1983), II, 959–960.

19. D. Edmond Hiebert, *The Epistle of St. James* (Chicago: Moody, 1979), p. 311.

20. Benedict, "Oaths," p. 959.

that the swearer decides upon, the speaker has gone too far. God's judgment will come, not only upon those who speak falsely but also upon those who use His name inappropriately.

Questions for Discussion

1. What sins of the rich did James denounce?
2. What are the different ways that patience reveals itself?
3. In what ways was Job a patient man?
4. What is wrong with taking an oath?

13

Sickness and Sinning

James 5:13–20

Illness, accident, and physical disability are problems for almost everyone sooner or later. Even those who are unusually healthy and accident-free will experience the ailments and declining strength of old age, unless illness or accident ends life sooner.

This feature of human life sometimes becomes a special problem for Christians. Through their reading of the Bible, they learn that Jesus and His apostles healed the sick. What is sometimes overlooked is the fact that the apostles, at least, did not heal *all* the sick (2 Tim. 4:20). Christians may also remember that the Bible contains promises about healing and prayer. If one prays for healing in response to God's promise in Scripture, why does healing not always occur? It cannot be God's fault, so it is often concluded that the failure is lack of faith on the part of the sufferer.

Questions among suffering Christians have provided an opening for religious healers with their simplistic message that "God doesn't want you to be sick." A few passages of Scripture may be strongly emphasized and others completely ignored. Any failures to achieve total healing are blamed upon the weak faith of the victims and rarely upon the inadequacies of the healer or failure to understand the whole counsel of God upon the matter.

Sad indeed are some instances of believers who trusted God for

185

a miracle of healing that never came. The disillusionment of sincere Christians who have been taught to expect something from God, which apparently it was not His will to give, can be devastating to fragile faith. Bitterness and despair combine to increase the suffering and create confusion and doubt among families and friends. The disillusioned disciple is often less responsive to further truth than the uncommitted.

The Epistle of James contains one of the key biblical passages on sickness and healing. It has been studied, misapplied, and abused, but it has also been the source of great hope and encouragement to others who have carefully considered its teaching.

B. Prayer for the Sick (5:13–18)

Does verse 13 belong with the preceding section or with what follows? Some have understood the thought in the passage to be that one should not frivolously swear in times of adversity, but he should rather pray. Recognizing this logical connection to the previous discussion as a good transition, one is still better advised to see verse 13 as structurally parallel with verse 14. The clearly parallel constructions, "Is anyone suffering? . . . Is anyone cheerful? . . . Is anyone sick?"—followed in each instance by an exhortation, "Let him . . ."—forces the interpreter to regard these verses as part of the same paragraph.

1. The method to be used (5:13–14)

VERSE 13. "Is anyone among you suffering?" The verb *kakopathei* is broader than just illness and refers to the experiencing of various hardships and distresses. They can be mental and emotional as well as physical. The word means "to suffer misfortune."[1] The other New Testament occurrences of the term describe Paul's

---

1. Wilhelm Michaelis, "*Pascho*," TDNT, V, 936.

imprisonment in Rome (2 Tim. 2:9) and challenge Timothy to expect hardships in his ministry (2 Tim. 4:5). The cognate (*kakopatheias*) described the Old Testament prophets' experiences (James 5:10).

In the midst of adversity, the Christian's duty is to pray. It is not suggested that the only kind of praying is to request deliverance. It is also appropriate to pray for strength to endure. Prayer in its highest sense of communion with God and adoration of Him must recognize His hand in all aspects of life.

"Is anyone cheerful?" This question directs the attention to another of life's legitimate conditions. No blame is pronounced upon this condition of merriment, any more than upon the experiencing of hardship. What is urged is a proper communion with God in all of life's situations. "Let him sing praises." The verb *psalletō* meant "to sing," usually to the accompaniment of a harp. It cannot be restricted to the singing of Davidic psalms (see KJV), but its usage in the New Testament is confined to the praising of God in sacred music (Rom. 15:9; 1 Cor. 14:15; Eph. 5:19). James's reminder is probably directed to the fact that occasions of merriment and high spirits can easily be led off into sensuality and sin, and hence perspective is best retained by having God at the center of our thoughts. Praising God in song is, of course, a form of prayer.

VERSE 14. "Is anyone among you sick?" James now turns to physical illness. The verb *asthenei* indicates a serious condition, as its other New Testament uses reveal. It described a royal official's son who was about to die (John 4:46–47). It was used of Lazarus, who shortly did die (John 11:1–3, 6); of Dorcas, who also died shortly after (Acts 9:37); and of Epaphroditus, whose sickness brought him close to death (Phil. 2:26–27). An illness serious enough to cause a bedfast condition is implied by the statement "raise him up" in verse 15, and perhaps also by the note that the elders will "pray over him."

When one of the believers is seriously ill, he is directed to summon the elders of the church, and they are to pray over him.

Several details should be especially noted. The sick person himself is to take the initiative; others do not do it for him. It is the church leaders who are called, not persons with special gifts of healing (1 Cor. 12:9, 30). Nor are these persons priests, as the Catholic Douay Version mistakenly translates.[2]

In addition to praying for the sick one, and probably before doing so,[3] the elders are to anoint him "with oil in the name of the Lord." The disciples had done this during our Lord's ministry under His direction (Mark 6:13). Because the verb "anoint" used here is *aleiphō* rather than *chriō,* some attempt to distinguish them sharply. Lenski, for example, insists that a better translation would be "oiling with oil" because *aleiphō* is the general term for anointing of any kind, in contrast to *chriō,* the term commonly used of sacred anointings.[4] However, such a distinction cannot be maintained in all cases, as Hiebert has clearly demonstrated.[5] The general term *aleiphō* is sometimes used in the LXX with the sacred sense of anointing the priests (Exod. 40:15; Num. 3:3). The other verb (*chriō*) has been found in the papyri with regard to camels, and the cognate noun is used of lotion for a sick horse.[6] Hence it cannot be insisted that *aleiphō* has no sacred connotations.

The "oil" (*elaiōi*) is a commonly used olive oil, employed in that day for a great variety of purposes. One of its frequent uses was therapeutic. In the parable of the good Samaritan, the Samaritan applied oil and wine to the wounds of the robbery victim (Luke

2. The Greek term is *presbuterous,* not *hiereis.* Newer Roman Catholic versions, such as the Jerusalem Bible (1966) and the New American Bible (1970) have properly rendered it as "elders" or "presbyters."

3. The participle *aleipsantes* ("having anointed") is aorist, most commonly used to denote action prior to the main verb.

4. R.C.H. Lenski, *The Interpretation of The Epistle to the Hebrews and The Epistle of James* (Columbus: Wartburg, 1946), pp. 660–661.

5. D. Edmond Hiebert, *The Epistle of James* (Chicago: Moody, 1979), pp. 320–321.

6. James Hope Moulton and George Milligan, *The Vocabulary of the Greek Testament Illustrated from the Papyri and Other Non-Literary Sources* (Grand Rapids: Eerdmans, 1930, repr. ed.), p. 21.

10:34). Josephus records that Herod the Great was given a bath in a tub of warm olive oil during his last illness as a possible cure.[7] This acknowledged fact has led some to see only a medicinal use of the olive oil here.[8] However, it is asking too much for one to regard first-century Christians as so naive as to imagine that olive oil was the best medicine for every situation, regardless of the particular ailment.

Those who regard the oil as sacramental likewise go beyond the language of the text. The promise of healing is not attributed to the sacred qualities of the oil but to the prayer of faith (5:15). The well-known Catholic practice of delaying this anointing until the approach of death (extreme unction), for the purpose of securing forgiveness of sins, was a gradual development based on this passage. Yet that was clearly not the purpose in the mind of James, who gave this procedure for restoration to health, not in preparation for death. Not until the end of the eighth century is there any record in the church of anointing with oil to prepare for imminent death (except among a few Gnostic sects).[9]

The best understanding of the oil regards it as symbolic only, perhaps of the Holy Spirit, in light of other biblical terminology connecting "anointing" with "the Spirit" (Isa. 61:1; cf. Matt. 3:16; Luke 4:18; 1 John 2:20, 27). Herman A. Hoyt has written: "The oil becomes a beautiful symbol of the Holy Spirit who lives in and watches over the saint (Jas. 4:5). The vigilance of the Spirit is not merely for the spiritual welfare of believers but also extends to the physical body which is His temple."[10]

7. Josephus, *Jewish Antiquities,* 17, 172 (6.5), in The Loeb Classical Library, trans. Ralph Marcus (Cambridge: Harvard Univ., 1963), Vol. VIII, p. 451.

8. Donald Burdick writes: "it is evident, then, that James is prescribing prayer and medicine." "James," EBC (Grand Rapids: Zondervan, 1981), XII, 204.

9. J. B. Mayor, *The Epistle of St. James* (Grand Rapids: Zondervan, repr. 1913 ed.), pp. 170–173; James H. Ropes, *A Critical and Exegetical Commentary on the Epistle of St. James,* ICC (Edinburgh: T. & T. Clark, 1916), pp. 305–307.

10. Herman A. Hoyt, *All Things Whatsoever I Have Commanded You* (Winona Lake, IN: BMH Books, 1948), p. 45.

2. The results that follow (5:15)

A promise is given that the prayer offered at this time will restore the sick one to health. This prayer is termed literally "the prayer of the faith." Use of the article with "faith" would seem to particularize this faith in some way. It could mean "the faith" in the sense of the revealed body of Christian doctrine. Hence prayer that is in accordance with Christian teaching on sickness, sin, and praying will achieve this healing. Or it could mean "the faith" exercised by the sick person in calling for the elders, and by the elders in praying. Whichever specific sense James may have intended, the Bible is clear that true faith is always man's response to what God has revealed. It is not just optimism or unfocused hopefulness. It is rather a trust in what God has told us about Himself, His program, and His instructions for living. The "prayer of the faith" is thus the prayer that is offered in the belief that God keeps His promises and will accomplish His will.

"The Lord will raise him up." Clearly the anointing oil is no magic potion, nor is the human exercise of praying ultimately responsible for the healing. Faithful praying is effective (v. 16b) because it calls upon God to do the work. It is the Lord who will accomplish the restoration. Are there exceptions to this promise? What does one conclude about cases where prayer has been offered and anointing oil has been used, but the patient died? It must be recognized that James was not offering any bolder promises than Jesus Himself had given: "And all things you ask in prayer, believing, you shall receive" (Matt. 21:22). The key to understanding is to recognize the implications of "believing" and "faith." Our believing must be a believing of what God has told us in His Word, and this requires taking into account the whole counsel of God on any particular matter. As related to prayer, this means asking "according to His will" (1 John 5:14). We must not make demands of God beyond His will. His Word tells us of His ability to heal, of His intention to heal in some cases, but also of His plan to allow suffering to exist in other cases and to allow death eventually in all cases until the rapture. "Obviously, if we could claim healing for a Christian in every illness (as some faith healers do) then none should ever die."[11] God does answer prayer, and He does restore sick people—sometimes by prayer alone, sometimes after their being anointed with oil, sometimes through medicine or surgery, and sometimes by a combination of several or all of these means. Our praying "in faith" must accept all that He has revealed and trust His sovereign will for the rest.

The thought is then added that "if he has committed sins, they will be forgiven him." Inasmuch as James has already indicated that all have committed sins (3:2), and "if" in this statement must refer to sins that caused his illness. Physical illness may result from sin, and experience provides numerous examples. Venereal diseases, alcoholism, and narcotics addiction are a few of the obvious ones. The Bible also teaches that God may bring sickness as a discipline for sin (1 Cor. 11:29-30). Nevertheless, this is by no means always the case. Jesus taught the disciples that it was neither the sin of the victim nor that of his parents that caused the case of blindness (John 9:2–3). Thus James said "if" he has committed sins...." The possibility should be considered and opportunity given for confession, but it must not be assumed as true in every case. Even, however, in cases where sin was the direct cause, God is gracious, and sincere prayer will bring forgiveness so that guilt will not stand in the way of healing.

3. The need for confession and prayer (5:16)

Because sin is so pervasive in human life, there is continual need for both spiritual sensitivity and appropriate action where sin

---

11. E. William Male, "Divine Healing According to James 5," *Grace Journal* I, 2 (Fall 1960), p. 29.

has been committed. When sinning has occurred, the confession required here is not to a priest but "to one another." This passage is not sufficient warrant for an indiscriminate and continuing baring of the soul to others, with perhaps the temptation to outdo one's comrades in the number and magnitude of things confessed. It does suggest, however, that confession of specific wrongs should be made to those who have been wronged, and that sinfulness that was public and has tainted the whole church should be confessed before the church. Prayer likewise should be made on behalf of each other for forgiveness and healing. Such mutual prayer implies that those who have been confessed to are forgiving and are willing to pray for and restore a sinning brother or sister.

The exhortation is concluded with the encouraging word that prayer made by one whose sin has been removed is greatly effective. Translations of this oft-quoted promise vary because of the difficulty in rendering the participle *energoumenē* with "prayer." The King James Version gives it as "the effectual fervent prayer"; the New American Standard Bible has "the effective prayer," and the New International has "prayer . . . is effective." Whether the participle should be regarded as a passive, as Mayor insists in a lengthy discussion,[12] or as a middle, as Adamson argues carefully in a refutation of Mayor's analysis,[13] has been debated for many years.

Those who treat it as a passive explain the thought as "prayer that is made effective by the Spirit." It may be granted that such a concept is taught elsewhere (e.g., Rom. 8:26), but the absence of any reference to God or the Spirit as the energizing agent here weakens this explanation. It is sometimes argued that all nine New Testament examples of this verb in the middle/passive form are passive.[14] Adamson, however, has clearly shown that this is by

12. Mayor, *James,* pp. 177–179.
13. James B. Adamson, *The Epistle of James,* NICNT (Grand Rapids: Eerdmans, 1976), p. 199–200, 205–210.
14. Mayor, *James,* p. 178.

no means certain, and that it is far more likely that all nine are middles. He proposes the translation, "the prayer of a righteous man is very powerful in its operation."[15] Ropes gives the sense: "A righteous man's praying has great effect when he prays."[16]

4. The example of Elijah (5:17–18)

VERSE 17. Elijah was the fourth Old Testament figure to be used by James for illustration (Abraham, 2:21–24; Rahab, 2:25; Job, 5:11). Next to Moses, he was probably the most highly revered historical personage among first-century Jews. Elijah's name appears thirty times in the New Testament. James wished to use him as an example of effective prayer, but because he was so highly regarded by the Jews, it was necessary for the readers to be reminded that he was still just a human being "with a nature like ours." The Greek term *homoiopathēs* (translated "subject to like passions" in KJV) occurs one other time in the New Testament, where Paul used it to explain that he and Barnabas were "of the same nature" as the people of Lystra (i.e., human, not gods, Acts 14:15). The example of Elijah, therefore, was one to which any godly man should be able to relate.

Elijah prayed earnestly[17] for rain to cease, and his prayer brought a drought of three and one-half years in Palestine. The incident is recorded in 1 Kings 17:1, but the precise prayer is not given. However, prophets were understood to make their pronouncements on the basis of God's instruction, gained from communion with Him. Elijah stated that the authorization for his predication was the Lord God of Israel "before whom I stand."

15. Adamson, *James,* pp. 205–210.
16. Ropes, *James,* p. 309.
17. The rendering "prayed earnestly" regards *proseuchēi prosēuxato* ("with a prayer he prayed") as an intensive expression, similar to the Hebrew infinitive absolute.

A greater problem is the duration of the drought, which is stated to be "three years and six months," although no such time is recorded in the Old Testament. A time of "the third year" is mentioned in connection with Elijah's time at Zarephath during these days, and a total time of three and one-half years for the

Statue of Elijah slaying the prophets of Baal at Mount Carmel *Muhraqa*.

drought would not contradict this. It is significant that Jesus used the same computation as James for the length of Elijah's drought (Luke 4:25). In all likelihood this was a well-known fact of Jewish history, although it is not in the canonical Scriptures.

James Orr has suggested the time period to be computed as follows: When Elijah announced the drought, it was at the time when the rainy season should have begun (otherwise it would have been nothing unusual, since six months of no rain was normal before the rains resumed in the fall). Hence six months of drought may be added to the three years mentioned in 1 Kings 18:1, giving the total as Jesus and James both stated it.[18]

VERSE 18. The resumption of the rains occurred following the episode of Elijah with the prophets of Baal at Mount Carmel. Although the Old Testament text (1 Kings 18) does not specifically mention Elijah as praying for rain, it does depict his praying to God for fire from heaven (vv. 36–37). Mention is also made of Elijah's crouching down on the earth and putting his face between his knees in an obvious attitude of prayer while waiting for the rains to begin (vv. 41–46).

The point of James is clear: God answers prayer when righteous men pray. The efficacy is not in the prayer *per se,* or anointing oil (in the case of illness), or in the man himself (as though some were of a different nature or position than others), but in the God who has chosen to accomplish His will through His faithful and obedient children.

C. Converting a Sinner (5:19–20)

1. The sinner restored (5:19)

It would not be difficult to construe these final verses of the Epistle as a part of the discussion just preceding. However, the

18. James Orr, *The Bible Under Trial in View of Present-Day Assaults on Holy Scripture* (New York: Armstrong, 1907), pp. 264–265.

initial words, "my brethren" (*adelphoi mou*), are used at the
beginning of a sentence by James in only one other instance, and
this was clearly to introduce a new topic (2:1). Furthermore, one
would expect the close of the letter to offer some sort of summa-
tion of the contents, or at least a conclusion based upon the
material that has been given. It can be seen that these closing
sentences, while fitting easily with the previous discussion, form a
suitable conclusion to the themes introduced at the beginning of
the Epistle. James has been writing about the various temptations
and sinful actions that were going on in the church. This
concluding statement ties it all together and lays a responsibility
upon the church, as well as holding out an encouraging promise.

"If any among you strays from the truth" has its focus within
the Christian group. The direct address, "my brethren," also calls
for the same conclusion. After mentioning in the letter a great
many sins that Christians may commit (e.g., favoritism, uncontrolled
speech, judging one another, friendship with the world), James
indicates that such discussion was not to be taken merely as an
academic analysis of church conditions but as a call for action.
Those who had strayed from the truth of the gospel and its
attendant responsibilities needed to be brought back to proper
conduct. (Of course, the statement was also applicable to mere
professed believers who may have joined the group, but it was
certainly not intended primarily as a challenge to evangelism.)

To "turn back" the straying Christian is to turn him around
from his wrong direction. The King James rendering, "convert,"
suggests initial conversion to many readers, but this is an unnecessary restriction of the Greek term (*epistrepsēi*) and is not the
idea that the context would lead us to expect. The author is
talking about restoration to the truth, which had been violated.

2. The benefits achieved (5:20)

Two benefits are indicated. The first is that the restorer "will
save his soul from death." Although some interpreters explain

196

"his" as a reference to the restorer (i.e., will save his own soul),[19] it seems more plausible to this writer to refer it to the restored sinner. A more difficult problem is the identification of the "death" mentioned here. Does it refer to spiritual and eternal death, which the unconverted will experience if he is not brought to faith? This identification is often made by those who are influenced by the expression "save a soul" (*sōsei psuchēn*), as well as by the serious tone of the admonition. However, the Greek term *psuchē* ("soul") is often used in the sense of "life," as seen in the following instances: "... those who sought the Child's life [*psuchēn*] are dead" (Matt. 2:20); "... do not be anxious for your life [*psuchēi*], as to what you shall eat..." (Matt. 6:25).

Inasmuch as the words are addressed to Christian "brothers," the only ones at risk of eternal death would be mere professed believers, and these do not seem to be the major focus of James's instruction. Hence it is better to interpret "death" here as physical death. The context has been discussing physical illness and the possibility of sin being involved in it (5:15–16). The thought was that if sin were not confessed, healing would not occur, and presumably physical death would follow. The apostle Paul wrote of physical death as a divine discipline for the sins of Christians (1 Cor. 11:30–32). The case of Ananias and Sapphira must have also been well known in Christian circles (Acts 5:1–11).

A second benefit that comes from restoring a wayward Christian is that it "will cover a multitude of sins." In what sense does James mean that sins will be "covered" (*kalupsei*)? If the thought is that a non-Christian will be brought to repentance and faith, then this covering of sins may refer to forgiveness from God, as Psalm 32:1 states: "How blessed is he whose transgression is forgiven, / Whose sin is covered!" (The LXX used the same word, *epekaluphthēsan*, for "covered.") The "multitude of sins" would denote one's entire guilt of sins, which God will forgive to those who believe the gospel.

19. Adamson, *James,* p. 203. Most interpreters, however, refer it to the soul of the wanderer.

Another possibility, however, may be more probable. A similar phrase occurs in 1 Peter 4:8, "Above all, keep fervent in your love for one another, because love covers a multitude of sins." In that context, Peter was discussing love and forgiveness on the human level, stating that Christian love toward one another forgives and forgets and does not continually dredge up past sins and insist upon exposing them. It is quite possible that both Peter and James were drawing their thought and wording from Proverbs 10:12, "Hatred stirs up strife, / But love covers all transgressions." There the concept was clearly human love as acting to heal and restore. This latter explanation fits well with the understanding that the sinner in view is a Christian who has stumbled. It is the responsibility of the church through its mature members to restore such ones out of love (Gal. 6:1), thus preventing (it is hoped) a multitude of sins that might otherwise follow, as well as not unduly publicizing the sin that has just occurred.

With these clear and practical words, James ends his letter. Not even the customary greetings or other concluding instructions are allowed to intrude upon the message itself as he comes to the closing. He has demonstrated that Christian faith is a serious matter. It is not just a creed but a life-transforming experience that shows itself in action. It is a faith that works.

Questions for Discussion

1. Is it always God's will to heal the sick?
2. What is the relation between sinning and sickness?
3. Should anointing of the sick with oil be practiced today?
4. How widely and to whom should sins be confessed?
5. How does restoring a sinner cover a multitude of sins?

Bibliography

Adamson, James B. *The Epistle of James,* in The New International Commentary on the New Testament series. Grand Rapids: Wm. B. Eerdmans Publishing Co., 1976.

Alford, Henry. *The New Testament for English Readers.* Chicago: Moody Press, repr., n.d.

———. *The Ante-Nicene Fathers.* Vol. VIII. Edited by Alexander Roberts and James Donaldson. Grand Rapids: Wm. B. Eerdmans Publishing Co., repr. 1978.

Arndt, W. F. and Gingrich, F. W. *A Greek-English Lexicon of the New Testament.* Chicago: University of Chicago Press, 1957.

Barnett, A. E. "James, Letter of," *The Interpreter's Dictionary of the Bible,* E–J. New York: Abingdon Press, 1962.

Blaiklock, E. M. "Ships," *The Zondervan Pictorial Encyclopedia of the Bible.* Edited by Merrill C. Tenney. Vol. V. Grand Rapids: Zondervan Publishing House, 1975.

Benedict, Fred W. "Oaths," *The Brethren Encyclopedia.* Philadelphia: The Brethren Encyclopedia, Inc., 1983.

Burdick, Donald W. "James," *The Expositor's Bible Commentary.* Vol. 12. Grand Rapids: Zondervan Publishing House, 1981.

Calvin, John. "Commentaries on the Epistle of James," *Calvin's Commentaries.* Vol. XXII. Grand Rapids: Baker Book House, repr. 1979.

Cansdale, G. S. "Horse," *The Zondervan Pictorial Encyclopedia of the*

Bible. Edited by Merrill C. Tenney. Vol. III. Grand Rapids: Zondervan Publishing House, 1975.

Carr, Arthur. *The General Epistle of James,* in the Cambridge Greek Testament for Schools and Colleges series. Cambridge: University Press, 1896.

Davids, Peter H. *The Epistle of James,* in The New International Greek Testament Commentary series. Grand Rapids: Wm. B. Eerdmans Publishing Co., 1982.

———. "Theological Perspectives in the Epistle of James." *Journal of the Evangelical Theological Society* 23:2 (June 1980).

Deissman, Adolf. *Bible Studies.* Translated by Alexander Grieve. Edinburgh: T. & T. Clark, 1901.

Doerksen, Vernon. *James,* in Everyman's Bible Commentary series. Chicago: Moody Press, 1983.

Edersheim, Alfred. *Sketches of Jewish Social Life.* Grand Rapids: Wm. B. Eerdmans Publishing Co., repr. 1950.

Eusebius, *Ecclesiastical History.* Translated by Hugh Jackson Lawlor and John Ernest Leonard Oulton. London: Society for Promoting Christian Knowledge, 1927.

Girdlestone, Robert B. *Synonyms of the Old Testament.* Grand Rapids: Wm. B. Eerdmans Publishing Co., repr. 1948.

Guthrie, Donald. *New Testament Introduction, Hebrews to Revelation.* Chicago: Inter-Varsity Press, 1962.

Harris, R. Laird; Archer, Gleason L.; and Waltke, Bruce, eds. *Theological Wordbook of the Old Testament.* Chicago: Moody Press, 1980.

Harrison, Everett F. *Introduction to the New Testament.* Grand Rapids: Wm. B. Eerdmans Publishing Co., 1971.

Hiebert, D. Edmond. *The Epistle of James.* Chicago: Moody Press, 1979.

Hoyt, Herman A. *All Things Whatsoever I Have Commanded You.* Winona Lake, IN: BMH Books, 1948.

Johnstone, Robert. *Lectures Exegetical and Practical on The Epistle of James.* Grand Rapids: Baker Book House, repr. 1954.

Josephus, *Antiquities of the Jews.* Translated by Louis H. Feldman, in The Loeb Classical Library. Cambridge: Harvard University Press, 1965.

————. *Jewish Antiquities.* Translated by Ralph Marcus, in The Loeb Classical Library. Cambridge: Harvard University Press, 1963.

————. *The Jewish War.* Edited by Gaalya Cornfeld. Grand Rapids: Zondervan Publishing House, 1982.

Kittel, Gerhard, and Friedrich, Gerhard, eds. *Theological Dictionary of the New Testament.* Translated by Geoffrey W. Bromiley. Grand Rapids: Wm. B. Eerdmans Publishing Co., 1964–72.

Lange, John Peter, ed. *Commentary on the Holy Scriptures.* Grand Rapids: Zondervan Publishing House, reprinted.

Laws, Sophie. *A Commentary on The Epistle of James,* in Harper's New Testament Commentaries series. New York: Harper & Row, Publishers, Inc., 1980.

Lenski, R.C.H. *The Interpretation of The Epistle to the Hebrews and The Epistle of James.* Columbus: The Wartburg Press, 1937.

Lightfoot, J. B. *The Epistle of St. Paul to the Galatians.* Grand Rapids: Zondervan Publishing House, repr. 1965.

Male, E. William. "Divine Healing According to James 5." *Grace Journal* I, 2 (Fall 1960).

Mayor, Joseph B. *The Epistle of St. James.* Grand Rapids: Zondervan Publishing Co., 1913 repr.

Metzger, Bruce M. *A Textual Commentary on the Greek New Testament.* London: United Bible Societies, 1971.

Meyer, Arnold. *Das Ratsel des Jakobusbriefes.* Giessen: A. Topelmann, 1930.

The Mishnah. Translated by Herbert Danby. London: Oxford University Press, 1933.

Mitton, C. Leslie. *The Epistle of James.* Grand Rapids: Wm. B. Eerdmans Publishing Co., 1966.

Moulton, J. H., and Howard, W. F. *A Grammar of New Testament Greek.* Vol. II. Edinburgh: T. & T. Clark, repr. 1968.

Moulton, James Hope, and Milligan, George. *The Vocabulary of the Greek Testament.* Grand Rapids: Wm. B. Eerdmans Publishing Co., repr. 1972.

Oesterley, W. E. "The General Epistle of James," *The Expositor's Greek*

Testament. Vol. IV. Grand Rapids: Wm. B. Eerdmans Publishing Co., n.d.

Orr, James. *The Bible Under Trial.* New York: A. C. Armstrong and Son, 1907.

Perkins, Pheme. "Expository Articles: James 3:16—4:3." *Interpretation* 37:3 (July 1982).

Phifer, Kenneth G. "Expository Articles: James 2:1–5." *Interpretation* 36:3 (July 1982).

Plummer, Alfred. "The Epistle of James," *The Expositor's Bible.* Edited by W. Robertson Nicoll. Vol. VI. Grand Rapids: Wm. B. Eerdmans Publishing Co., repr. 1943.

Plumptre, E. H. *The General Epistle of St. James,* in The Cambridge Bible for Schools and Colleges series. Cambridge: University Press, 1909.

Reicke, Bo. *The Epistle of James, Peter, and Jude,* in The Anchor Bible. Garden City, NY: Doubleday & Company, 1964.

Robertson, A. T. *Studies in the Epistle of James.* Nashville: Broadman Press, n.d.

————. *Word Pictures in the New Testament.* Vol. VI. New York: Harper & Brothers, Publishers, 1933.

Ropes, James Hardy. *A Critical and Exegetical Commentary on the Epistle of St. James,* in The International Critical Commentary series. Edinburgh: T. & T. Clark, 1916.

Ross, Alexander. *The Epistle of James and John.* Grand Rapids: Wm. B. Eerdmans Publishing Co., 1954.

Scott, J. Julius. "James the Relative of Jesus and the Exception of an Eschatological Priest." *Journal of the Evangelical Theological Society* 25:3 (September 1982).

Sharp, Granville. *Remarks on the Uses of the Definitive Article in the Greek Text of the New Testament.* Philadelphia: B. B. Hopkins and Co., 1807.

Tasker, R. V. G. *The General Epistle of James,* in The Tyndale New Testament Commentaries series. Grand Rapids: Wm B. Eerdmans Publishing Co., 1956.

The Testament of Job. Edited by Robert A. Kraft. Missoula, MT: Scholars Press, 1974.

Townsend, Michael J. "Christ, Community and Salvation." *The Evangelical Quarterly* 53:2 (April 1981).

Vine, W. E. *Expository Dictionary of New Testament Words.* Grand Rapids: Zondervan Publishing House, repr. 1981.